Macintosh Slick Tricks

Macintosh
Slick Tricks

• • • • • • • • • • • • • •

Maria L. Langer

RANDOM HOUSE
ELECTRONIC PUBLISHING

New York

Macintosh Slick Tricks

Produced and composed by Parker-Fields Typesetters Ltd.

Published in the United States by Random House, Inc., New York, and simultaneously in Canada by Random House of Canada, Limited.

Manufactured in the United States of America

First Edition

0   9   8   7   6   5   4   3   2   1

ISBN 0-679-75606-X

Trademarks

New York   Toronto   London   Sydney   Auckland

To Laura and Norbert—
dreams can come true.

Contents

· · · · · · · · · · · · · · · · · · · ·

Acknowledgments

Writing a book may require long, lonely hours in front of keyboard, but getting the author's words and images on paper for readers to enjoy requires the efforts of many, many people. I'd like to thank a few of them here.

At Random House, I'd like to send out a big thanks to Tracy Smith for getting me involved in this project. As usual, it was a pleasure working with her. I hope to do it again soon!

Also at Random house, I'd like to thank Jean Davis Taft, Elizabeth LaManna, and the various editors and production people who worked on this book. You "behind-the-scenes" folks do a lot more than most people will ever know. I appreciate your efforts and thank you for putting together a fine book.

I'd also like to extend my thanks to Ralph Merritt for providing help and insight about Newtonland, Mike Bielen for creating a screen shot my poor old Macintosh IIcx could not produce, and Ian at TransNet for helping me purchase the Power Macintosh that'll put my IIcx in semi-retirement. Additional thanks go to the authors of *Macintosh Tips & Tricks* articles, especially Terry Wilson and Ron Baron, for helping me to fill each monthly issue with interesting and useful tricks.

I'd like to send out a big "group thanks" to the software developers and shareware authors who continue to produce such fine products for Macintosh users. I've mentioned a few of my favorites throughout this book.

Of course, I also need to thank Mike for letting me spend those long, lonely hours in front of a keyboard and for putting up with me when the final deadlines made me cranky and unreasonable. It's happened before and it'll happen again, but I appreciate his understanding each time it does.

Maria Langer
July 1994

Introduction

· ·

The *Slick Tricks* series is based on a simple idea: You don't have to know a lot about a computer or program to unleash its power and put it to work for you. By knowing a handful of useful, time-saving tips and tricks, you can get your work done faster and with much less effort than you might think.

Today's software—even the operating system software that comes with your Macintosh—is rich in features. Most people don't take advantage of the features that can help them most because they don't have time to page through manuals or work through lengthy, often pointless tutorial exercises. But beyond the software's interface lies a wealth of tricks you can master easily, without wading through thick volumes of software documentation. You can flip through the pages of this *Slick Tricks* book and find hundreds of tips, tricks, and shortcuts to make your work easier.

What Are Slick Tricks?

· ·

Each and every page of this book is full of tips, tricks, and shortcuts that make working on a Macintosh quicker, easier, and more productive.

Most of the tricks are either short statements describing a specific short-cut you can use to do something faster or sequences of steps you can follow to perform a more complicated task. Actual screen illustrations help guide you along the way. You'll find basic tricks you'll use all the time, like tricks for managing documents, customizing the interface, printing, and getting the most out of popular Macintosh applications. You'll also find more powerful customization tricks you can use to make your Macintosh look and work the way you want it to.

This book won't start from the ground up to teach you the basics, though. You'll need to be familiar with basic Macintosh operating procedures, like clicking, dragging, and using menus and dialog boxes, to get the most from this book. In addition, if you're still using System 6, it would be a good idea to upgrade before getting started, since many of the tricks in this book apply only to System 7 software. Otherwise, you'll miss out on some of the best tips this book has to offer.

What You Need to Use These Tricks

. . . .

What will you need to get the most out of this book? In most cases, nothing but your Macintosh, the software that comes with it, and the willingness to try things for yourself. Most of the tricks presented in this book will work with just about any Macintosh model running System 7 or later—*including* the new Power Macintoshes. And if you've got a PowerBook or Newton, you'll find a chapter just for you.

Your Macintosh system software is powerful, flexible, and full of hidden tricks that are covered within the pages of this book. It doesn't waste a lot of pages telling you how to use expensive utility software you might not have. But as you'll see throughout this book, there are a number of useful utilities you can use to get more out of your Macintosh. You'll learn what these utilities are and where you can get them—often for free!

Using a *Slick Tricks* Book

· ·

You can think of a *Slick Tricks* book as a cookbook—browse its pages and try out a "recipe" or two. Since these are fairly "right-brained" books, you may need to browse until you find the recipe you need. These short, friendly books can't possibly cover *all* the features of a system or program—if they did, you'd wind up spending more time wading through useless bits of information than learning the tricks you can really use.

Trick

You'll see a number of icons in a *Slick Tricks* book. A "Trick" is a hands-on procedure that shows you how to do something. A "Tip" gives you a helpful, general hint about how to approach a task or work out a solution to a problem. "Traps" tell you about procedures you should avoid. "Sidebars" provide background material for a particular topic.

Tip

Trap

Each *Slick Tricks* book follows the general conventions of the system or program it's about. You'll find the keys you need to press in boldface type and any text you need to type in sans serif type, like this: Press **Spacebar** and type Letter. If you need to press two keys at once, you'll see them with a hyphen between them, like this: Press **Command-S**. You'll see lots of keyboard shortcuts throughout this book because using the keyboard is often faster than choosing from a menu.

Sidebar

Let's Get Started!

· ·

That's enough of an introduction. You can figure out the rest as you go along—there's nothing really complicated. Turn the page and start learning how you can tap the hidden power of your Macintosh.

Macintosh Slick Tricks

Chapter 1

· ·

Finder Tricks

This chapter covers a wide variety of tricks you can use in the Finder—the program that creates the desktop interface of your Macintosh. Some of these might seem extremely basic if you've been using a Macintosh for a while, but even experienced Macintosh users will find plenty of treasures tucked away in this chapter.

Keyboard Shortcuts and Other Tricks

· ·

One of the toughest things for new Macintosh users to get used to is the mouse. After a little practice, however, mousing around will become second nature. Still, which do you think is quicker, using your mouse to select a menu command or pressing two or more keyboard keys together? If you'd like to reduce the number of times you need to reach for your mouse as you work, this section is for you.

1

Use Your Keyboard to Choose a Menu Command

Keyboard shortcuts for menu commands are among the most basic of Macintosh tricks. Because of standardization among the Macintosh operating system and most applications, many of the menu shortcuts are the same from program to program. This makes them easy to re-member. But even if you can't remember them, don't worry. The menus themselves provide a cheat sheet of keyboard shortcuts:

1 Use your mouse to pull down any Finder menu, like the **File** menu shown in Figure 1.1.

2 Note the keystroke indicators down the right side of the menu for most of the commands. Pressing one of these keystrokes performs the command mouselessly. So, for example, you can press **Command-O** to open a selected icon since that's the shortcut for the File menu's Open command.

Use Extended Keyboard Keys for Menu Commands

If you have an extended keyboard (one with the Function keys along the top), you may prefer to use the first four function keys for Edit

File	
New Folder	⌘N
Open	⌘O
Print	⌘P
Close Window	⌘W
Get Info	⌘I
Sharing...	
Duplicate	⌘D
Make Alias	
Put Away	⌘Y
Find...	⌘F
Find Again	⌘G
Page Setup...	
Print Window...	

Figure 1.1 Keyboard shortcuts on the Finder's File menu

What Those Symbols Mean

The Finder uses the Command key (symbolized by ⌘) for all keyboard shortcuts that appear on its menus. In other programs, however, you may see other symbols for other keys. Here's a complete list:

⌘	Command Key
⌥	Option Key
⌃ or ^	Control Key
⇧	Shift Key
↵	Return Key
⌅	Enter Key
⌫	Delete Key
␣	Spacebar

If you're wondering what the ellipsis (...) character after some command names is all about, it signifies that choosing the command will display a dialog box. Commands without the ellipsis work without displaying any dialog box—or any chance to cancel them.

menu commands. These keys work in many (but not all) Macintosh applications:

F1	Undo
F2	Cut
F3	Copy
F4	Paste

Use the "Secret" Keyboard Commands

Not all keyboard shortcuts are documented on the Finder's menus. Apple provides four built-in FKEYs that you might find useful:

◆ Press **Command-Shift-1** to eject the floppy disk in the internal floppy drive. This is an especially useful command when your Macintosh is locked up or busy with another task and you can't eject a disk any other way. If you have two floppy disk drives, **Command-Shift-1** ejects the disk in Drive 1 and **Command-**

Shift-2 ejects the disk in Drive 2. (There's more on ejecting disks later in this chapter.)

♦ Press **Command-Shift-0** to eject the floppy disk in an external floppy disk drive (if one is connected).

♦ Press **Command-Shift-3** to create a picture in PICT format of your entire screen. This screen shot, which is saved to your startup disk, can be opened with TeachText version 7.0 or later, SimpleText, or any other graphics program.

 ### Use Your Keyboard to Select Icons

On a System 7 Macintosh, you can also use your keyboard to select icons on the Desktop or in an open Finder window.

♦ Press a letter key to select the first icon with a name beginning with that letter. For example, pressing **S** selects the file called "Statement" in Figure 1.2. (If no icon name begins with the letter you pressed, the icon with a name that follows that letter alphabetically is selected.)

♦ Press **Tab** to select the next icon alphabetically. In Figure 1.2, if "Statement" is selected and you press **Tab**, "TeachText" becomes selected. You can also press **Shift-Tab** to move backward alphabetically.

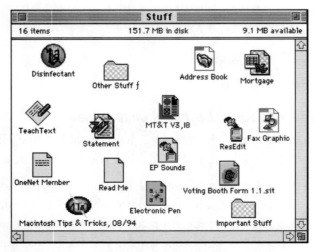

Figure 1.2 Working with icons in Icon view

♦ Press an arrow key to move from one selected icon to the next one to its right, left, top, or bottom. In Figure 1.2, if "Statement" is selected and you press **Right Arrow**, "MT&T V3,I8" becomes selected. (The Right Arrow and Left Arrow keys work in icon views only.)

Use Your Keyboard to Rename Icons

Once you've selected an icon, you can use your keyboard to rename it.

1 Press **Return** or **Enter** while an icon is selected to select its name. This is illustrated in Figure 1.3.

2 To change the name, type in a new name while the entire name is selected.

3 To move the insertion point to the end of the name, press the **Right Arrow** key while the entire name is selected or the **Down Arrow** key while the insertion point is within the name. To move the insertion point to the beginning of the name, press the **Left Arrow** key while the entire name is selected or the **Up Arrow** key while the insertion point is within the name.

4 To move the insertion point one character at a time, press the **Right** or **Left Arrow** key while the insertion point is within the name.

5 To accept the name change, press **Return** or **Enter** while the insertion point is within the name.

Use Your Keyboard to Open Icons

Once an icon is selected, you can use your keyboard to open it or its parent folder.

♦ Press **Command-Down Arrow** to open a selected icon. (This is the same as pressing **Command-O** which activates the **Open** command on the **File** menu.)

Figure 1.3 Selecting an icon name

♦ Press **Command-Up Arrow** to open the window that the current window is in (it's "parent" folder or disk). For example, if the "Stuff" folder were inside the "Documents" folder, pressing **Command-Up Arrow** while the "Stuff" window was open would open the "Documents" folder.

♦ Press **Command-Shift-Up Arrow** to make the Desktop active.

Use Your Keyboard to Expand and Collapse Outlines

The keyboard also lets you expand and collapse outlines in list views.

♦ Press **Command-Right Arrow** to expand the outline of a folder. This is shown in Figure 1.4. Press **Command-Left Arrow** to collapse a selected, expanded folder.

♦ Press **Command-Option-Right Arrow** to expand all levels of an outline of a selected folder. Press **Command-Option-Left Arrow** to collapse all levels of a selected, expanded folder.

Use Your Keyboard to Scroll Through Finder Windows

If you have an extended keyboard (the one with the function keys along the top), you can use your keyboard to scroll through Finder windows displayed in List view.

Figure 1.4 Working with icons in List view

♦ Press **Page Up** or **Page Down** to scroll the window contents up or down.

♦ Press **Home** to view the first group of files in the window.

♦ Press **End** to view the last group of files in the window.

These keys also work in directory list windows inside **Open** and **Save As** dialog boxes. Note that pressing one of these keys does not select an item—it only changes the window view.

Use Your Keyboard in Dialog Boxes

You can use some keystrokes to select buttons and navigate through folders inside the dialog boxes displayed by many applications. Here's a list of keystrokes that you can try:

Keystroke	Results
Enter (and often **Return**)	Chooses the default button (the one with the dark border around it).
Esc or **Command-.**	Chooses the **Cancel** or **Close** button.
Up or **Down Arrow** keys	Selects previous or next item in a directory window.
Page Up or **Page Down**	Displays the previous or next windowful of information in a directory window.
Home or **End**	Displays the first or last windowful of information in a directory window.
Command-Up Arrow	Selects parent folder in a directory window.
Command-Left Arrow or **Command-Right Arrow**	Displays the contents of the previous or next mounted disk in a directory window.
Tab	Moves from one edit box to the next in most dialog boxes; moves from directory list to name edit box in a directory window.

Command-D	In a directory dialog box, displays the desktop level (the same as clicking the **Desktop** button).
Letter key	Choose the first file or folder beginning with that letter in a directory window.

In some applications, pressing the key that corresponds to the first letter on a button chooses that button. For example, in a dialog box with buttons for **No**, **Yes**, and **Cancel**, pressing **N** chooses **No**. In other applications, you may need to hold down the Command key while pressing the letter key for this to work.

Use the Type-Ahead Buffer

Your Macintosh can store up to 20 keystrokes in a buffer. It does this when it's busy performing other tasks (like saving a file, sending a file to the printer, or opening a dialog box), so you don't have to wait until it finishes.

You can use this feature to your advantage by entering keystrokes you know your Macintosh will expect. For example, say you want to print two copies of pages 1 through 3 of a document. With the document open, use the keystrokes listed on the left side of the following table without bothering to wait for your Macintosh to catch up. The right side of the table explains what each keystroke does.

Command-P	Opens the **Print** dialog box
2	Enters **2** in the **Copies** box
Tab	**Moves to the From** box
1	Enters **1** in the **From** box
Tab	Moves to the **To** box
3	Enters **3** in the **To** box
Return	"Clicks" **Print**

Don't Overtype the Buffer

If you type more than 20 characters ahead, your Macintosh will loose some of the characters you type, beginning with the first ones. In other words, your Macintosh remembers only the last 20 characters you type. So don't type too much while your Macintosh is busy doing other things.

Option Key Tricks

In the Finder, holding down the **Option** key often changes the way menu commands and mouse actions work. Sometimes, you can even see the command name change on the menu. For example, hold down **Option** and pull down the Finder's **File** menu. Back in Figure 1.1, the second command was **Close Window**. In Figure 1.5, however, you can see how the command changes to **Close All**. In this section, you'll find some ways the **Option** key can change a command.

Figure 1.5 The File menu with the Option key held down

Close All Windows

Hold down **Option** and choose **Close All** from the **File** menu to close all open Finder windows. This also works if you hold down **Option** while clicking in the topmost window's Close box. If you prefer to do this mouselessly, press **Command-Option-W**.

Open One Window While Closing Another

Hold down **Option** and choose **Open** from the **File** menu to open a selected icon and close the window the icon is in. This also works if you hold down **Option** while double-clicking an icon. If you prefer to do this mouselessly, press **Command-Option-O** or **Command-Option-Down Arrow**.

You can also do this in reverse. **Press Command-Option-Up Arrow** to open the parent folder of the current window while closing the current window.

Empty the Trash Quickly

Hold down **Option** and choose **Empty Trash** from the **Special** menu to delete the contents of the trash without seeing a warning dialog box. This also makes it possible to delete locked files without unlocking them first.

Clean Up Icons

The **Clean Up Window** (or **Clean Up Desktop**, depending on which is active) command on the **Special** menu organizes icons, or small icons, neatly within a window by moving them into the nearest available space in an invisible grid. Figure 1.6 shows a "cleaned up" version of the same window we saw in Figure 1.2. (If you want to organize only a few icons in a window, select the icons first, then hold down the **Shift** key while choosing **Clean Up Selection** from the **Special** menu.)

Holding down the **Option** key while pulling down the **Special** menu changes this command to **Clean Up by Name**, **Clean Up by Date**, **Clean Up by Size**, or **Clean Up by** any other **View** menu option. This makes it possible to organize icons neatly in alphabetical, date, size, or other order.

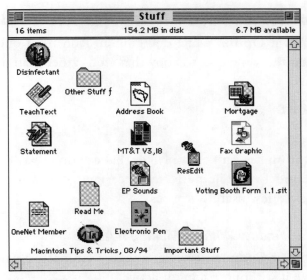

Figure 1.6 **A cleaned up window**

How do you specify which **Clean Up** option should appear? Try this example to **Clean Up by Kind**:

1 Choose **by Kind** from the **View** menu. The active window's icons organize alphabetically by the type of icon (application, control panel, document, system extension, etc.).

2 Choose **by Icon** from the **View** menu. The active window's icons appear as icons in the window.

3 Hold down **Option** and pull down the **Special** menu. The **Clean Up** command should read **Clean Up by Kind** since **by Kind** was the last view you used before switching to Icon view.

Not only does the **Option** key make it possible to organize icons by a certain view, but it also moves the icons closer together. It does this by moving icons into the first invisible grid spaces they fit into rather than the grid spaces closest to their original position.

Zoom a Window to Fill Your Screen

Hold down **Option** and click in a window's **Zoom** box to zoom the window to almost full screen size. The rightmost side of the screen remains uncovered by the window so you can still get access to disks and the trash.

Copy an Icon to a Different Location on the Same Disk

Hold down **Option** while dragging an icon from one window to another on the same disk to copy that icon rather than move it.

Command Key Tricks

The **Option** key isn't the only key that can do tricks. Holding down the **Command** key while performing certain actions with the mouse can also yield a few useful surprises.

Move a Window Without Making It Active

Hold down **Command** while dragging an inactive window's **Title** bar to move it without making it active.

Display a Window's Secret Menu

Hold down **Command** while clicking on the title of a window in its **Title** bar. A menu showing the path to that window appears. This is illustrated in Figure 1.7. To make another window in that path active, choose it from the menu.

Reverse Grid Settings

Hold down **Command** while dragging an icon to temporarily reverse the **Always Snap to Grid** settings in the **View** control panel. (More on the View control panel later in this chapter.)

Multiple Icon Tricks

Sometimes you need to work with more than one icon at a time. This section has some tips for selecting and moving multiple icons.

Figure 1.7 A window's secret menu

Shift-Click to Select Multiple Icons

Hold down the **Shift** key while clicking on each icon you want to select. You can also deselect one or more already selected items by holding down the Shift key while you click on them.

Draw a Selection Box to Select Multiple Icons

Use your mouse pointer to "drag" a selection box around the icons you want to select. You can see an example of this in Figure 1.8. Any icon that is even partially inside the selection box will be included in the selection.

Select All Icons in a Window

Choose **Select All** (**Command-A**) from the **Edit** menu. This selects all the icons in a window.

Select Almost All Icons in a Window

If there are 20 icons in a window and you need to select, say, 18 of them, do you Shift-click on each one? You could, but there's a better way. Try this:

1 Choose **Select All** (**Command-A**) from the **Edit** menu to select all the icons in the window.

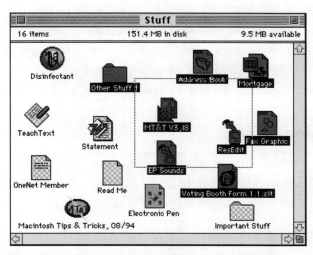

Figure 1.8 Dragging a selection box to select icons

2 Hold down **Shift** and click on the icons you don't want included in the selection.

Use Outline Views to Select Icons in Different Folders

If you need to select a group of icons but they're in different folders, an outline in a List view can help. Here's how:

1 Open the window containing the folders with icons you want to select.

2 If the window is not in a List view, choose any option *except* **by Small Icon** or **by Icon** from the **View** menu.

3 Click on the triangle icon before the folders containing the icons you want to select so that the triangle points down and the folder opens as part of an outline. Do this for each folder containing an icon that you want to select. When you're finished, all icons should be displayed. You may have to use the vertical scroll bar to see them all.

4 Hold down **Shift** and click on each icon you want to select. Use the scroll bar if necessary to see and click on them all. The results are illustrated in Figure 1.9.

Move or Copy Multiple Icons

Once you've selected multiple icons, you can drag all of them by dragging only one. Use your mouse to "grab" one of the selected icons (be sure you are not pressing the **Shift** key when you grab it or you may deselect it) and drag it to a new destination. When you let go of your mouse, all selected icons will move to the new location.

View Customization Tricks

• •

The **Views** control panel (illustrated in Figure 1.10) lets System 7 users customize window views and the commands on the **View** menu.

Change File Name Size

Use the font and font size pull-down menus to change the way file-names appear in windows. Having trouble reading the default 9-point

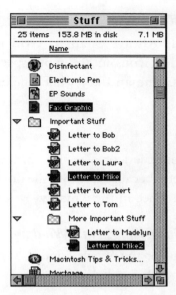

Figure 1.9 **Selecting icons in different folders**

Geneva font? Make it bigger! You can type just about any number into the font size edit box. Just be aware that a large font size might cause part of a filename to get cut off in List views.

Choose a Straight or Staggered Grid

Use radio buttons to choose a **Straight** or **Staggered Grid for Icon** views. Staggered grid is especially useful if the files displayed in icon view have long names.

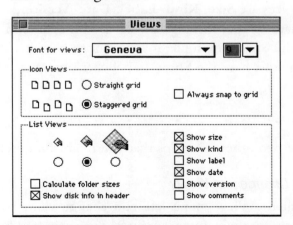

Figure 1.10 **The System 7 Views control panel**

Turn Snap to Grid On or Off

Click the check box beside **Always Snap to Grid** if you want your Macintosh to always position icons in an empty space on its invisible grid. (Holding down the **Command** key while dragging an icon temporarily reverses this setting.)

Pick a List View Icon Size

Use radio buttons to choose the icon size to appear in list views. The middle size is especially useful because it shows the document's real icon yet does not take up much space in the window.

Determine What Information Displays in a Window

Check boxes at the bottom of the Views control panel let you determine what should show in each window.

♦ **Calculate Folder Sizes** displays the total size of files within a folder. While this might be useful, keep in mind that it can also slow down your Macintosh since folder sizes must be calculated each time you open a List view window containing folders.

♦ **Show Disk Info in Header** displays the number of items in the folder, the amount of disk space used by all items on the disk, and the amount of disk space available.

♦ The other **Show** check boxes let you determine what information is provided to the right of each filename in the window. Choices are **Size**, **Kind**, **Label**, **Date**, **Version**, and **Comments**. Whatever you turn on here also becomes an option in the **View** menu. So, for example, if you want to be able to view **by Label**, you must have the **Show Label** check box turned on here.

Other View Tips

Here are two other View tips that you might find useful.

Click to Change List Views

Although the **View** menu lets you change views, you might find it quicker to change a List view in an open window by clicking on the header you want to view by. For example, if you are viewing a window **by Name** and want to view **by Date**, click on the **Date** header in the window to instantly change views. Notice that the header you are viewing by appears underlined.

Specify New Folder Views

A new folder's size and view is determined by its parent folder. So, if you need to create a number of new folders inside a folder, you can determine in advance what the new folders' sizes and views will be by changing the parent folder's size and view first. Then, when you choose **New Folder** (**Command-N**) from the **File** menu, all the new folders have the desired settings. After the folders have been created, you can always change the parent folder back to the size and view you want for it.

Label Tricks

System 7 users can use the **Labels** control panel (see Figure 1.11) to customize the labels that appear under the **Label** menu and in list views (with the **Show Label** option turned on in the **Views** control panel). Here are some tricks for changing the label name and color and using labels effectively.

Customize Labels

Customizing the seven labels in the **Labels** control panel is easy. Simply select the name of the label you want to change and type in a new name. It can be anything you like. As shown in Figure 1.12, you will see your changes in the **Label** menu immediately.

Figure 1.11 The Labels control panel

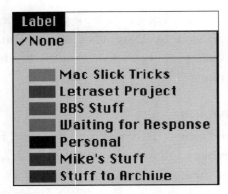

Figure 1.12 A customized Label menu

Change Label Colors

If you have a color Macintosh, you can also change Label colors. Here's how:

1 In the **Labels** control panel, double-click on the color sample beside the label you want to change. A standard Macintosh color wheel like the one in Figure 1.13 appears.

2 Select a new color by clicking on it within the color wheel. You can change brightness by sliding the vertical scroll bar up or down.

3 Click **OK** to accept your change and close the color wheel window.

View by Label Sorts in Label Order

Some people think that the **by Label** command under the **View** menu displays window contents sorted by the name of the label. This isn't so. **By Label** sorts in the same order the labels appear under the **Label** menu. If you have more than one item with the same label, those items are then sorted in alphabetical order by name.

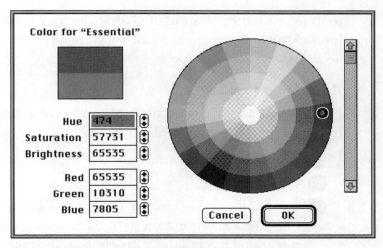

Figure 1.13 The standard Macintosh color wheel

Sound Tricks

The Sound control panel, which is illustrated in Figure 1.14, lets you select the system alert sound. Here are some sound tricks you can try with it.

Turn Off the Sound

If you work in a library—or in an office just as quiet as one—you might want your Macintosh to keep its sounds to itself. To turn off the System sound, open the Sound control panel and drag the sliding volume bar

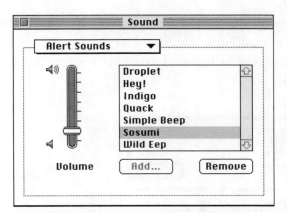

Figure 1.14 The Sound control panel

to its lowest setting. Instead of making a peep, your menu bar will flash inversely (white words on black background) when your Macintosh needs to get your attention.

Record Your Own Sound

If you've got a microphone attached to your Macintosh you can use it to record your own custom alert sounds.

1 Open the Sound control panel.

2 Click **Add**.

3 A recording dialog box like the one in Figure 1.15 appears. Click the **Record** button to begin recording a sound. Whatever sound reaches the microphone will be recorded.

4 Click **Stop** to stop recording the sound.

5 Click **Play** to play back the sound. If you're not happy with the sound you've recorded, repeat Steps 3 through 5 until you are.

6 Click **Save**.

7 Enter a name for the sound in the edit box and click **OK**.

8 After a moment, the sound name will appear in the Sound control panel's main window. You can choose that sound for your alert sound by clicking on it to select it.

Get Info Tricks

The **File** menu's **Get Info** command (**Command-I**) offers information about the selected disk, file, or folder. An example of the **Get Info** window is illustrated in Figure 1.16. This window lets you perform a few tricks, too.

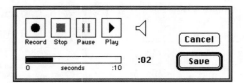

Figure 1.15 Recording a sound with the Sound control panel

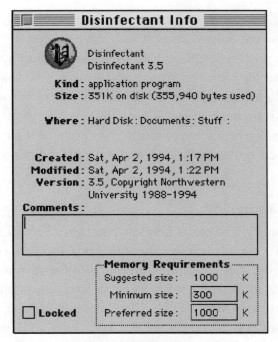

Figure 1.16 The Get Info window for an application

Add Finder Comments

The **Comments** area of the **Get Info** window lets you enter any comments you like about a file. You can use this to provide information about the file for yourself or for other file users. Since it's possible to view **by Comments**, you can also use this area to enter information you may want to sort by for a window's list view.

Get Info Comments Can Be Lost!

Rebuilding the Desktop, which is covered in Chapter 9, deletes all comments from the **Get Info** window. Keep this in mind if you use the Comments feature.

Lock Files

The **Locked** check box lets you lock a file so that it can't be changed. Use this to protect template documents from being overwritten. If you try to save a file with the same name, you will be told that you can't. You can also use this to prevent applications from becoming infected by viruses—just be aware that it is *not* a foolproof virus protection method. In addition, locking an application may prevent it from working since some applications actually read and write to their own files as you use them.

Make Stationery

The **Stationery Pad** check box lets you turn a regular document into a template. To use this feature, check this box and then open the file with the application that created it. Although different applications treat stationery pads in different ways, in most cases, the stationery pad document will be opened as an "Untitled" document. This will force a **Save As** dialog box even if you choose the **Save** command, thus making it a bit tougher to accidentally overwrite the original stationery pad document.

Set an Application's RAM Allocation

The **Get Info** window also enables you to set the RAM allocation for applications. Enter a value in the appropriate edit box and close the **Get Info** window. When you launch the application, it will use the RAM you specified. This is covered in much greater detail in Chapter 4.

Stop the Trash Warning

One of the most annoying features of System 7 is the trash warning that appears when you empty the trash: "The Trash contains 1 item. It uses 6K of disk space. Are you sure you want to permanently remove it?" To get rid of this annoying message, do this:

1. Click once on the **Trash** icon to select it.
2. Choose **Get Info** (**Command-I**) from the **File** menu.
3. Turn off the check box for **Warn Before Emptying**, as shown in Figure 1.17.
4. Close the **Get Info** window.

Figure 1.17 Turning off the trash warning

Change the Icon

System 7 users can also use the **Get Info** window to change the icon for one file, folder, or disk to the icon for another file, folder, or disk. It's as simple as copy and paste. Here's how:

1 Click once on the icon you want to use to select it.

2 Choose **Get Info** (**Command-I**) from the **File** menu.

3 Click once on the icon in the **Get Info** window to select it. A box appears around it.

4 Choose **Copy** (**Command-C**) from the **Edit** menu. The icon is copied to the clipboard. Close the **Get Info** window.

5 Click once on the icon you want to replace to select it.

6 Choose **Get Info** (**Command-I**) from the **File** menu.

7 Click once on the icon in the **Get Info** window to select it. A box appears around it.

8 Choose **Paste** (**Command-V**) from the **Edit** menu. The icon in the clipboard is pasted over the current icon. When you close the **Get Info** window, the icon is changed.

You can also paste icons into the Scrapbook to store them for later use.

To restore an icon to its original shape, simply click on the icon in the **Get Info** window and press the **Delete** key.

Ejecting vs. Unmounting Disks There is a definite difference between ejecting and unmounting a disk. When you *eject* a disk, it is physically removed from the Macintosh. That doesn't mean your Macintosh has forgotten all about it—it may ask you to reinsert the disk. When you *unmount* a disk (normally by dragging its icon to the trash), you tell your Macintosh to forget the disk exists. Your Macintosh will not ask you to reinsert it.

Here are some additional considerations:

- When you unmount a floppy, the disk is also ejected.
- You must unmount a SyQuest cartridge before you can physically eject it from the SyQuest drive.
- You cannot unmount the startup disk.
- You can unmount non-startup disks, including external hard disks, but you may see a message informing you that the drive will reappear when you restart.

Disk Ejection Tricks

Earlier in this chapter, you saw that **Command-Option-1** (and **Command-Option-2** on a two-floppy Macintosh) can eject a disk. Here are a few more disk ejection tips.

Avoid the Eject Disk Command

The **Special** menu's **Eject Disk** command (**Command-E**) ejects a floppy disk. What you might notice, however, is that after the disk has been ejected, its grayed image remains on the desktop. This is because the disk has been ejected but not unmounted. Your Macintosh may display an annoying message like the one in Figure 1.18 asking you to insert

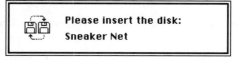

Please insert the disk:
Sneaker Net

Figure 1.18 The dreaded insert disk message

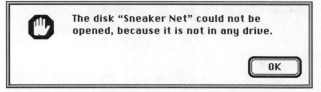

Figure 1.19 What your Macintosh says when it can't find a disk

the disk. This is especially bothersome if it happens after you've mailed the disk to your company's regional sales office in Sydney, Australia.

Dismiss the Insert Disk Message

The insert disk message that appears when your Macintosh asks you to insert a disk that wasn't unmounted (see Figure 1.18) is particularly frustrating since it doesn't offer any options other than to insert the disk. Here's a secret: You can usually press **Command-.** to dismiss the message. This might generate another message, like the one in Figure 1.19, but at least you can click **OK** for that one. If the insert disk message reappears, be persistent—press **Command-.** again. Your Macintosh usually gives up and unmounts the disk.

Choose Put Away to Eject a Disk

Choose **Put Away** (**Command-Y**) from the File menu to eject and unmount a selected floppy or other non-startup disk.

Chapter 2

• •

Filing Tricks

Having trouble keeping track of your files? Tired of digging through folders to find applications and documents? Think backing up is too much of a chore to do regularly? This chapter may solve all these problems for you by providing tricks you can start using now to take control of your files.

File Naming Tricks

• •

What's in a name? With up to 31 characters, there can be quite a bit in a Macintosh filename. Here are some file naming tips and tricks to help you find files when you need them.

 ### Save Files with Descriptive Names
Which document name is more descriptive, "Letter" or "ABC Co. Job Cover Letter 10/16"? While "Letter" could be a letter about anything, "ABC Co. Job Cover Letter 10/16" is probably the cover letter accompanying a resumé for a job at ABC Co. that was written on 10/16.

Those 30 characters really can tell a story. Take advantage of every character your Macintosh allows. Here are some suggestions:

♦ For letters, name the file with the name of the person the letter is addressed to and either the subject or date (or both if you can). Some examples include: "Tracy Smith, Contract 7/16," "Tom H, New Business 5/18," and "Town of Cresskill, Dog License."

♦ For files related to a specific project, include the name of the project as part of the filename. This is especially useful if you don't keep these files together in the same folder. Some examples include: "Slick Tricks Outline," "Slick Tricks Chapter 01," "Slick Tricks Chapter 11," and "Slick Tricks Acknowledgments." (Note that when you include a leading zero in a filename that includes a number, you can keep 2-digit numbers in order. "10" comes before "2" alphabetically, but after "02.")

♦ If you use a fax modem to send documents, you may want to include the word "fax" in the filenames of documents you send by fax. This way, when reviewing correspondence sent to a particular person, you can immediately identify which of the documents were faxes sent to that person's fax machine.

There's one important exception to this tip: naming files that will be used on IBM-compatible computer systems. If you're working with files that will ultimately be used by DOS or Windows users, you should follow DOS naming conventions. You can read more about that in Chapter 5.

Include Dates in Filenames

While your Macintosh can keep track of the dates that a file is created and modified and display the modification date in a List view Finder window, you might find it useful to include a date in a filename anyway. This helps you to identify it in directory dialog boxes, like the one that appears when you open a file from within an application. For example, in Figure 2.1, can you tell which is the most recent letter to Norb L?

Colons in Filenames

You can use any character in a filename except the colon (:). Your Macintosh reserves this character for use in *path names* (the complete name of a file, including parent disk and folders). If you type a colon while naming a file, your Mac will either ignore it or automatically convert it to a hyphen, depending on the application.

Establish and Stick to a Standard File Naming Convention

Using standard words, phrases, or even codes in filenames can make them easy to find when you need to. For example, if the name of every report you write contains the letters "RPT," you can use the Macintosh's built-in search feature—the **Find** (**Command-F**) command under System 7's **File** menu or the **Find File** desk accessory under System 6's **Apple** menu—to find all the documents containing those characters, that is, all of your reports.

Force Filenames to the Top or Bottom of Alphabetical Lists

Directory dialog boxes like the one in Figure 2.1 and Finder windows viewed by Name display files in alphabetical order. Sometimes, however, you might want a specific file to be at the beginning or end of the list. Rather than beginning these files with the letters A or Z (which is often

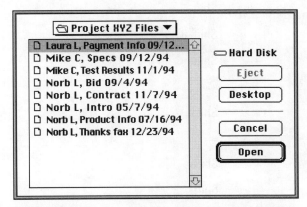

Figure 2.1 Dates in filenames can be helpful in directory dialog boxes

impractical), use invisible or nonalphabetic characters. For example, the space character (which is invisible) comes before most other characters alphabetically. Naming a file " Fax Template" rather than "Fax Template" (note the space in the first example just before the letter F) will force it to the top of the list. Use as many additional leading spaces as you like. If you want a file to appear at the end of a list, use a character that comes after the normal alphabetic characters, like the bullet (•) character (**Option-8**).

Table 2.1 shows some suggestions in alphabetical order. The list on the left includes characters that appear before the uppercase letter A. The list on the right includes characters that appear after the lowercase letter z.

There are more characters available, of course, but these are probably the most useful for beginning filenames since they're somewhat graphic in nature. Keep in mind that although these characters are standard, they do not appear in all fonts. They are included in Geneva (the standard system font that can be changed in the Views control panel under

Table 2.1 Characters Used to Position a Filename in a List

Character before A	Keystroke	Character after z	Keystroke
	Spacebar	†	Option-T
!	Shift-1	•	Option-8
#	Shift-3	≠	Option-=
*	Shift-8	∞	Option-5
+	Shift-=	±	Option-Shift-=
-	-	√	Option-V
<	Shift-,	Δ	Option-J
=	=	«	Option-\
>	Shift-.	»	Option-Shift-\
?	Shift-/	…	Option-;
@	Shift-2	◊	Option-V

System 7) and Chicago (the standard font used in dialog boxes and menus). When you type a character that is not included in a font, it will either appear as a plain box or not appear at all.

Document Management Tricks

Naming files is only a small part of document management. The way you organize your files on disk can make a real difference in how quickly you can locate a specific file when you need it. While everyone has his or her own personal filing system, you may find the tips in this section helpful when setting up or fine-tuning your system.

Organize Files by Project

If you use your Macintosh to work on a variety of different projects, you may find that organizing files by project makes it easy to find files fast. For example, say you have three current projects: Project A, Project B, and Project Q. Create a folder for each project and store the files related to each one in the appropriate folder. If you have a lot of files for Project Q, you may want to create subfolders within the Project Q folder—say, for Correspondence, Financial Workups, Drawings, Work in Progress, Finished Work, or a combination of these. The kind of work you do will determine the way you organize files within each project folder.

Use a Miscellaneous Folder

If you often create documents that are not related to any specific project, store them together in one folder. Think of it as the "Miscellaneous" drawer of a file cabinet.

Use List Views to Organize Files

The Finder offers a number of List views to view the contents of windows (check Chapter 1 for more details). You can even view different windows with different views. A folder full of correspondence to one specific person or organization may be best viewed **by Date** so that the most recent documents come to the top of the window. A folder full of miscellaneous documents for a variety of projects may be best viewed

by Name. If you use your Macintosh's Label feature (which was also discussed in Chapter 1), you may want to view the contents of certain folders **by Label**. Icon view and Small Icon view are useful if you like to group icons manually within a window. Remember, you can view any window using any option under the **View** menu.

Don't Save Documents with Applications!

Many Macintosh users—especially new ones—fall into the trap of saving documents in the folder containing the application that created them. For example, if a document was created with Microsoft Word, these folks save it in the same folder as Word and its accompanying files. Why? Because when they use the **Save** or **Save As** command, the default folder (the one that appears in the directory window of the **Save As** dialog box) is the one that contains the Microsoft Word application.

New Macintosh users often don't know that they can use this dialog box to open and save in other folders. More experienced Macintosh users might be just plain lazy.

This is not a good way to organize files for several reasons:

♦ To find a file, you must remember which application you used to create it. If you have only a few applications, this might not be a big deal, but when you've got a variety of different applications you use regularly, keeping track of which one you used for each document can be quite a chore.

♦ If you're working on a project with files created with several different applications, those files are scattered throughout your hard disk, making them difficult to find and keep track of.

♦ When you install a new version of an application, it may install a brand new folder on your hard disk. If you're not careful, you may discard your documents when you throw away the folder containing the previous version.

♦ Scattering documents all over your hard disk makes files difficult to back up efficiently. You'll learn more about backup strategies later in this chapter.

Save Temporary Files on the Desktop

If you need to save a file that you expect to discard a short while later, save it on the Desktop. This makes it easy to find the file when you want to delete it. It also makes it tough to forget that the file exists since it's right out in the open for you to see.

System 7 users can save files to the Desktop easily by clicking the **Desktop** button in a **Save As** dialog box just before clicking the **Save** button (see Figure 2.2). System 6 users cannot save directly to the Desktop, but they can move files out of disks and folders and leave them on the desktop.

Create a Folder on the Desktop

To create a folder on the desktop, choose New Folder (Command-N) while no windows are active.

Put Away Files on the Desktop

Choose **Put Away** (**Command-Y**) from the **File** menu to move a selected file on the Desktop back into the disk or folder it came from. You can find out where a file came from by choosing **Get Info** (**Command-I**) from the **File** menu and looking at the **Where** field of the **Get Info** window that appears.

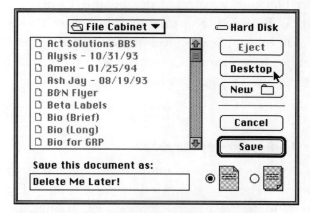

Figure 2.2 The Desktop button in a Save As dialog box

Application Management Tricks

If you have more than just a handful of application software packages on your Macintosh, you probably realize that managing all this software and the files that go with them can be quite a task. Like document management, there is no right or wrong way to organize your programs so they're easy to find and use. Here are a few tips you might find useful when developing your own method.

Store Applications Together

While no one says you can't store applications on the main level of your startup volume, storing them in folders inside an all-purpose application folder is a good way to keep them organized. It also keeps your hard disk's main window neat, like the one in Figure 2.3.

Don't Combine the Files of Several Applications in One Folder

If you store more than one application in the same folder, be sure to create a separate folder for each application. Why? Because if you combine applications and their support files in one folder, you might find it tough to tell which files belong to which application. When it's time to upgrade software and you want to throw the old version's support files out, you might not be able to figure out which ones should be discarded. Not only that, but there's a slight chance that more than one application may use a file with a specific name. Since you cannot have more than one file with the same name in a folder, one of the files may get deleted on installation.

Group Applications by Purpose

If you have lots and lots of applications, you might want to group them by purpose. The hard disk window illustration in Figure 2.3 illustrates a separate folder for general applications, utilities, and telecommunications software. You might want to go a step further and create separate

Figure 2.3 The real-life hard
disk of an organized person

folders for each of the kinds of application software packages you use,
like word processing, business, and graphics. Your goal should be to
limit the number of files and folders inside of each folder while avoiding
filling your hard disk's main window with folders. It's a delicate balance
to create, but once you set up a system, it'll make finding specific applications easy.

Put a Drag-and-Drop Folder on Your Desktop

If you use System 7's drag-and-drop feature to open files or perform
specific tasks, consider keeping drag-and-drop applications (or aliases of
them—more on that later in this chapter) in a folder and leaving that
folder on your Desktop, perhaps right beneath your hard disk icon.
Then, when you need to use one of these files, double-click on the
folder to open it and display the applications.

There are two main benefits to keeping these files in a folder rather
than loose on your desktop:

♦ Keeping files in a folder on your Desktop keeps your Desktop
   neat and makes the files easy to find.

♦ You can view the contents of a folder by any option under the
   View menu. Use Small Icon view or a List view and make the
   window long and narrow to limit the amount of desktop space
   the files take up when the folder is open. Figure 2.4 shows an
   example.

Figure 2.4 A drag-and-drop folder's contents in Small Icon view

Alias Tricks

In the days before System 7, if you wanted to open a file or folder, you had to locate it on the disk and either double-click its icon, or select it and choose **Open** (**Command-O**) from the **File** menu. Finding the actual file or folder was also required to open it from within an application. System 7's alias feature changed all this by making it possible to create an alias or "pointer" file. Open the alias and you open the file or folder it points to. You can make as many aliases of a file as you like and place them anywhere on your hard disk or desktop. This makes it very convenient to find and open often-used files.

This section tells you how you can create aliases and provides some tips and tricks for using them.

Make and Use Aliases

To make an alias of a file or folder, follow these steps:

1 Find the file or folder you want to create an alias for, and click once on it to select it.

2 Choose **Make Alias** from the **File** menu. After a moment, an icon appears near the original file. It has the same icon and name, but the name appears in italic characters and includes the suffix "alias." You may also notice that the filename

appears in an edit box so that you can type in a new name immediately. This is shown in Figure 2.5. If you want to change the name at this point, type a new name in and press **Return**. Just remember that it can't be the same name as the original while both are in the same folder.

3 Drag the file to a new location. (Chances are that if you bothered to create an alias, you don't want to keep it in the same location as the original.)

4 If you want to give the alias the same name as the original, do it now. Click on the name area. When the edit box appears around the name, type in a new name and press **Return**.

Aliases Are Not Copies!

An alias is *not* a copy of a file. It is a *pointer*—it points to the file. Double-clicking an alias does not open the alias. It opens the file that the alias points to.

This is very important to remember if you want to copy a file. Dragging an alias to another disk copies the alias, not the original file. If you copy an alias onto a floppy disk and give the disk to someone else, an error message like the one in Figure 2.6 will appear when that person tries to open it on his Macintosh. Be sure to copy the original file for use on another Macintosh.

Finding the Original File

If you can't remember where an alias's original file is, use **Get Info** to find it.

1 Click once on the alias to select it.

Figure 2.5 An alias icon

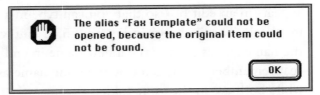

Figure 2.6 What your Macintosh displays when it can't find an alias's original file

② Choose **Get Info** (**Command-I**) from the **File** menu. The **Get Info** window appears, as shown in Figure 2.7.

③ Click the **Find Original** button. Your Macintosh displays the window containing the original icon with its icon selected.

Leave Aliases on Your Desktop

Your Desktop is one good place to leave alias files (you'll see another in the next section of this chapter). Create aliases for the applications, documents, control panels, desk accessories, and folders you use most

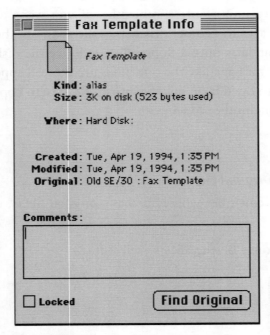

Figure 2.7 The Get Info window for an alias

often and arrange them in a row across the bottom of your screen. If you size your Finder and document windows so that they don't block this area, they'll always be easily accessible.

Don't Clutter Up Your Desktop!

 Keeping aliases and other icons on your desktop makes it convenient to find and use them, but the law of diminishing returns applies: As icons proliferate, cluttering up your desktop, they take longer and longer to find. Try keeping them in a folder on your Desktop, as suggested for drag-and-drop applications earlier in this chapter. Or put them in the other good place: the Apple Menu Items folder.

Apple Menu Tricks

System 7 turned the Apple menu into something really useful, not just a place to store seldom-used desk accessories. By placing files into the Apple Menu Items folder inside the System Folder, you can add virtually anything to the Apple menu. This gives you immediate access to files you'd otherwise have to dig through folders to find. This section provides some tips and tricks for using the Apple menu.

 ### Put Aliases in the Apple Menu

Are there certain programs or files that you use every day? If so, the Apple menu is a perfect place to put them. But rather than put the actual file into the Apple Menu Items folder, put an alias of the file there. Why? Several reasons:

♦ Some applications must reside in the same folder as their support files. If you put one of these applications into the Apple Menu Items folder, the application may not be able to find the support files it needs. Error messages and inconsistent behavior may result.

♦ If you're trying to maintain a consistent organization strategy for your files, placing only some of them in the Apple Menu Items folder probably won't fit into your strategy. As a result, you may have trouble remembering exactly where files are located on disk and some files may get missed when making backups.

Remove Unused Desk Accessories from the Apple Menu

Apple's System Software Installer automatically installs desk accessories in the same old place it always installed them: under the **Apple** menu. But under System 7, you don't have to keep them there. You can use a desk accessory no matter where it is installed.

Do yourself a favor—delete the Apple-provided desk accessories you never use, like the Puzzle and the Notepad. Move the ones you use once in a while to another folder where you can find them when you need them. This shortens your Apple menu and makes more room for the files and folders you access most often.

A quick note for System 6 users: Don't be afraid to delete desk accessories you don't use. Use Font/DA Mover to remove unwanted desk accessories from your System file.

Use Folders in the Apple Menu

As you add more and more items to your Apple menu, the menu becomes longer and longer until it can't fit on your screen. This reduces the efficiency of the Apple menu by forcing you to scroll all the way down the menu to choose items at the bottom.

You can use folders in your Apple menu just as you use folders on your hard disk to organize files. Apple provides a good example: the Control Panels folder. Choose it from the Apple menu and the folder opens. Use folders to organize items under your Apple menu by category, type, or purpose. Use them to group the items you usually use together. This helps keep the length of the Apple menu within reason.

The Benefit of a Hierarchical Apple Menu

What Apple *should* have done when it programmed the Apple menu is make it into a hierarchical menu, one with pop-out menus displaying the contents of each folder. Although Apple didn't do this, other software developers did. *NowMenus*, a component of *Now Utilities* by Now Software, Inc. does this and much more. You might want to check into this and other hierarchical menu utilities if you find yourself making extensive use of the Apple menu.

Customize the Order of Items in the Apple Menu

The items on the Apple menu always appear in alphabetical order. You might find it more useful, however, to put the items you use most often at the top of the menu. That's easy enough to do—check the File Naming Tricks section at the beginning of this chapter for details on how you can cheat the alphabet.

Add Separators to Your Apple Menu

If customizing the order of items in your Apple menu isn't enough for you, you can also add separators.

1 Open your Apple Menu Items folder.

2 Choose **New Folder** (**Command-N**) from the **File** menu.

3 A new folder appears. Change the name of the folder so that it begins with a character that will position it alphabetically where you want a separator line to appear. After that first character, complete the name with either period characters or hyphens. Both are illustrated in Figure 2.8.

4 Repeat Steps 2 and 3 for as many separators as you want to add.

Pull down the Apple menu to admire your handiwork. It might look something like the illustration in Figure 2.8.

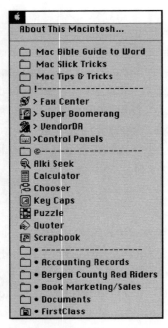

Figure 2.8 Separators
added to the Apple menu

Customize the Puzzle

If you decide to keep the Puzzle desk accessory, you might consider changing the picture on it for a new challenge each time you play with it. It's easy to do:

1 Use the **Copy** (**Command-C**) command to copy a black-and-white or color PICT image onto the Clipboard from within any application. For best results, it should be at least the same size as the Puzzle area.

2 Open the Puzzle.

3 Choose **Paste** (**Command-V**) from the **Edit** menu. The image is resized to fit into the Puzzle area.

Some additional points:

♦ To remove a custom picture from the Puzzle, choose **Clear** from the **Edit** menu.

♦ To switch from the Apple logo puzzle to a number puzzle, choose **Clear** from the **Edit** menu when the Apple logo puzzle is displayed. To go back to the Apple logo, choose **Clear** from the **Edit** menu when the number puzzle is displayed.

Disk Tricks

Hard disks, floppy disks, SyQuest cartridges, Bernoulli drives, CD-ROM disks, optical storage—the list goes on and on. How do you keep track of the files stored on these disks? How do you protect them from damage? How do you use them efficiently and effectively? The answers to these questions are here in this section.

Disk Labeling and Cataloging Tools That Won't Break Your Budget

If you're interested in inexpensive software to help you manage files stored offline, consider these two shareware gems:

- *Loodle* is a disk labeling utility created by Josh and Nick Franco that automatically reads floppy disks as you install them, and creates nice looking labels that print on standard label stock. It also includes a HyperCard stack that you can use to keep track of all those disks and files. Loodle is a shareware program that you can find on many online services and bulletin board systems.

- *FileList+* is a disk cataloging utility created by Bill Patterson that automatically reads floppy disks as you install them, and keeps a complete list of all files and their volumes (disks). It can also read higher-capacity media like SyQuest cartridges, hard disks, and even CD-ROM drives. *FileList+* is shareware—send the author what you think it's worth if you use it. You can find it on many online services and bulletin board systems.

Organize and Catalog Offline Files

If you store files offline—on floppy disks, removable media like SyQuest cartridges, or even hard disks that you don't regularly mount on your Macintosh—organize them the same way you organize files on your hard disk so they're just as easy to find. Label floppy disks so you know what's on them. Print a list of the contents of files and folders on removable media and hard disks, and store the lists with the media.

Don't Trust Important Files to Floppy Disk!

Of all storage media, floppy disks are perhaps the most fragile. Their plastic cases aren't always enough to protect them from magnetic fields, heat, dust, moisture, and the banging around they get inside briefcases, purses, and envelopes. Even when stored properly in a protective case, floppy disks sometimes just go bad. And, when they do, data can be lost forever.

Never trust a floppy disk to store the only copy of an important file. If you must store an important file only on a floppy disk, store another copy on another floppy disk. This goes for documents as well as your original program disks. Although program disks can be replaced, it sometimes take days or weeks for the replacement to arrive. What do you do while you're waiting? To be on the safe side, make backup copies of all original program disks before you install the software.

Use the Finder to Duplicate Disks

The **Special** menu's **Eject Disk** command (**Command-E**) ejects a floppy disk. As discussed in Chapter 1, however, after the disk has been ejected, its grayed image remains on the desktop. This makes it possible to copy one disk to another. Here's how:

1. With a floppy disk you want to copy inserted in the disk drive, choose **Eject Disk** (**Command-E**) from the **Special** menu.
   The floppy disk is ejected but its image remains on the desktop.

2 Insert a blank disk of the same capacity into the disk drive. If it hasn't been formatted yet, let your Macintosh format it when it offers to.

3 Drag the grayed image of the disk you ejected onto the disk you inserted. This tells your Macintosh to copy one disk's contents onto the other disk.

4 When your Macintosh asks if you're sure you want to completely replace the contents of one disk with the contents of the other disk, click **OK**.

5 Your Macintosh ejects the blank disk and prompts you to insert the original or "source" disk. Insert it. A progress box appears on the screen to indicate reading progress. Your Macintosh then ejects the source disk and prompts you for the blank or "destination" disk. Insert it. The progress box indicates writing progress. You may have to switch disks more than once, depending on the disk capacity and your Macintosh's installed RAM.

6 When the copying is done, the gray source disk image remains on the desktop, along with the destination disk's icon. The destination disk is in the drive. You can eject (or unmount) either disk by dragging its icon to the trash.

Lock Original Program Disks

Most software comes on floppy disks. To help protect your investment from being accidentally overwritten or damaged by a computer virus, lock original program disks before inserting them into your Macintosh. This makes it impossible for your Macintosh to write any information to the disk.

You can find the floppy disk lock on the back of the disk. Hold the disk with the sliding metal door facing down and you'll see the disk lock in the upper-left corner. Slide it up (open the hole) to lock the disk. Slide it down (close the hole) to unlock the disk. If you have trouble sliding the lock tab, insert the tip of a ballpoint pen in the tiny half-moon-shaped hole near the top.

Spring Cleaning Tricks

The original Macintosh hard disks were seldom larger than 10 or 20 megabytes. Imagine that! Most people have System folders bigger than that these days.

Although hard disks are getting bigger and bigger, they seem to be shrinking. Often, there's hardly enough room for all the files you accumulate. But therein lies the key: accumulation. Do you ever throw away the files you don't really need? This section will help you find and remove old files so you can make room for new ones.

View by Date to Find Old Files

Possibly the quickest way to find the oldest files in a folder is to choose **by Date** from the Finder's **View** menu. This sorts all files by their last modification date, putting the oldest at the bottom.

Use the Find Command to Find Old Files

System 7 users can find old files with the **Find** command.

1 Choose **Find** (**Command-F**) from the **File** menu.

2 Click the **More Choices** button to expand the dialog box.

3 From the first pop-up menu, choose **Date Modified**.

4 From the second pop-up menu, choose **Is Before**.

5 Use the arrows beside the date to change the date to the newest file you want to find. Your Macintosh will look for files *older* than the date you select. When you're finished, the dialog box should look something like the one in Figure 2.9.

6 If you want your Macintosh to display all found files at once, turn on the **All at Once** check box.

7 From the **Search** pop-up menu, choose the location to be searched. If you want to search a specific folder and its subfolders, make that the active window *before* you choose the **Find** command and it will appear on the list.

8 Click **Find**. Your Macintosh looks for files matching the date criteria you set and displays them.

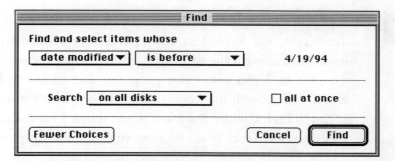

Figure 2.9 Using the Find dialog box to find old files

⑨ If you didn't have the **All at Once** check box turned on, choose **Find Again** (**Command-G**) from the **File** menu to find each file, one at a time.

Store Seldom-Used Files Offline

Often you'll have files on your hard disk that you need to keep, but you don't need to use on a regular basis. When free hard disk space becomes tough to find, these files should be the first to go. Store them on other storage media, like floppy disks, SyQuest cartridges, or spare hard disks. This way they're available when you need them, but are not taking up space better used by the files you need on a regular basis.

Delete Applications You Seldom Use

If your hard disk is playing host to one or more applications you rarely use, free up some space by deleting the applications. You may be surprised by how much space an application takes up. You can always reinstall from the original program disks when you need to.

The same holds true for programs you no longer need after a certain date. Income tax programs are a great example. The 1994 version of MacInTax takes up 7.5 MB of hard disk space, not to mention the fonts it installs in your System. Who knows how much disk space it'll eat up in 1995? When April 16 rolls along, delete this program. Also be sure to delete old versions of programs you update. No need to keep old software around.

Find and Delete TeachText

TeachText, the Apple text editor, is often provided with software and installed automatically on your hard disk when the software is installed. Trouble is, if you install five programs and all five include TeachText, you'll end up with five copies of it. No one needs more than one copy of TeachText. Choose the **Find** (**Command-F**) command from the **File** menu to find TeachText and remove all copies except one.

Store Applications and Documents on Removable Media

If you've got access to a high-capacity removable-media disk drive, like a SyQuest or Bernoulli drive, use it to store applications and documents you use together. Say, for example, that you use a page layout program like QuarkXPress or PageMaker to create a monthly newsletter and an occasional flyer. Rather than install the application on your hard disk (PageMaker 5.0 takes up 17 MB of hard disk space!), install it onto the removable media. Store all the files you create with that program on the same cartridge or disk. Then, when you need to work with that program, pop in the cartridge and get to work.

Defragment Your Hard Disk

Your Macintosh tries to store each file you save on disk in one piece on a contiguous area of disk space. After a while, however, it's forced to break files into multiple pieces, either because a file is resaved with more information than the last time it was saved or because there's simply less contiguous disk space available. This is called *fragmentation* and it's a normal occurrence. Your Macintosh can keep track of all the pieces of every file on disk. But accessing a file saved in five pieces takes more time and effort than accessing a file saved in only one piece. This slows down your Macintosh's operation. When more than 5 percent of the files on a disk are fragmented, the slowdown can become very noticeable.

To help cut down on the time it takes your Macintosh to run programs and open and save files, you can defragment your hard disk. This process takes all the file pieces and moves them around on disk until they're all reassembled properly. Unfortunately, Apple doesn't provide software to do this. That gives you two options if you want to defragment your disk.

- Use the Finder to copy all the files from your hard disk to another disk or set of disks. Then reformat your hard disk and copy all the files back onto it. As you can imagine, this can be quite a chore. But it's free and it does work.

- Use a defragmenting or optimizing utility software package. Some popular ones include *CP Optimizer* (part of Central Point Software's *MacTools*), *Speed Disk* (part of Symantec Corporation's *Norton Utilities for Macintosh*), and *Disk Express* (part of ALSoft, Inc.'s *ALSoft Power Utilities*). While it might not be worth the cost of these packages just to defragment your hard disk, all three include other useful disk utilities.

Backup Tricks

You back up your hard disk regularly, don't you? Well? The sad truth of the matter is that most computer users don't back up their files until *after* they lose information. They learn their lesson the hard way. Don't let this happen to you!

This section covers a few backup tricks that can help make backing up software less of a chore. Perhaps it'll even encourage you to do it more regularly!

Use the Find Command to Find New Files Created Since the Last Backup

In the "Use the Find Command to Find Old Files" trick described in the "Spring Cleaning Tricks" section earlier in this chapter, you saw how you could use **Find** (**Command-F**) to locate old files. You can follow almost the same exact steps to locate new files created since your last backup. Rather than choosing **Is Before** in Step 4, choose **Is After**. Then set the date in Step 5 to the date of your last backup. The files your Macintosh finds are the files that haven't been backed up yet.

Don't Back Up Applications

Unless you have plenty of backup media, don't bother backing up applications. Why? You should be able to reinstall all applications from their original program disks in the event of a problem. In fact, since many programs tend to store support files (preferences files, fonts, etc.) inside your System Folder these days, it's actually *better* to reinstall a program from the original disks than from a backup. This assures that all the files the program needs to run are properly installed where they should be.

What if you have a backup drive the same size as the drive you use for your day to day work? By all means, duplicate your hard disk on that. In the event of a hard disk crash, it's certainly easier to plug in another drive and keep working than to reinstall software and documents from backup disks.

Store Documents and Applications Separately

Documents stored separately from applications are much easier to back up. Simply drag the document folder icon onto your backup media icon and let the Finder do the rest. Even if you're forced to back up to floppy disks—don't worry, you're not the only one—it's much easier to drag file icons onto floppies when they're all located in the same place on your hard disk.

Back Up Important Documents Frequently

If you back up all your documents on a weekly basis, great! That's better than most people. But what about documents that you work on every day, like long reports, complex spreadsheets, or even chapters of a book? A few day's worth of changes could take days to reproduce if the originals were lost—if you could reproduce them at all. If you're working hard on files for an important project, back those files up at the end of each day. It should be a simple matter of dragging file or folder icons to a floppy disk. That's another reason why organizing files by project, which we discussed at the beginning of this chapter, is such a good idea.

Use Compression Software on Backups

If you've got lots of files to back up but are stuck with floppy disks or other low-capacity media, compression software may help by enabling you to fit more information on each disk. Although Apple doesn't provide compression software for the Macintosh, other companies do. There are two kinds of software to consider:

♦ Standard compression software like Aladdin Systems' *StuffIt Deluxe*, Bill Goodman's *Compact Pro*, and Now Software, Inc.'s *Now Compress* can help you squeeze more files onto disks, whether you want to back up the files, store them offline, or simply free up more hard disk space.

♦ Backup software products like Central Point Software's *CP Backup* (part of Central Point Software's *MacTools*), Fifth Generation Systems Inc.'s *FastBack Plus*, and Symantec Corporations's *Norton Backup* (part of the *Norton Utilities for Macintosh*) have file compression built in. That means they compress files automatically as they back them up. They also have other useful features that help make backing up easier to do.

Store Backups Away from Your Computer

Once you've backed up your files, store them in a safe place away from your computer. Why? Because if your computer is destroyed by a fire, flood, or some other major catastrophe, your backup files will probably be destroyed, too. Don't take chances.

Chapter 3

· ·

System Tricks

Macintosh System software is unique in the world of computers because it provides resources and instructions that other software uses—things like dialog boxes, windows, and error messages. In a way, it stands between the hardware and the application software, enabling them to communicate.

This chapter provides you with tricks for installing the System software and making it slimmer, trimmer, and faster. You'll also find a few simple customization tricks to help you give your Macintosh some personality.

Installation and Upgrade Tricks

· ·

The System software comes on a number of disks, complete with an Installer that makes installation easy. There are a few installation tricks you can take advantage of to make sure your System has only the components you really need. This may reduce the System's RAM requirements, leaving more RAM for your applications. You'll find those tricks, as well as tips for upgrading to a new version of the System software, in this section.

Start Your Computer from the Install Disk

If you're installing System software on your startup disk, you'll have to start your Macintosh with the first Install disk. Depending on the version of System software you're using, this disk could be labeled **Install**, **Install 1**, or even **Utilities 1** (System 6). The System software that comes with PowerBooks sometimes has a disk called **Install Me First**.

Do a Custom Install

Apple's System Software Installer offers a number of options. Most people take the easy way out and click the **Install** button in the **Easy Install** window (see Figure 3.1) that automatically appears. This won't hurt your Macintosh, but it will install a lot of files you probably don't need. This increases the size of the System heap (the amount of RAM the System requires to run), thus reducing the amount of RAM available for your applications. It also uses up additional disk space (although not much). The **Customize** button lets you override the Installer's recommended installation.

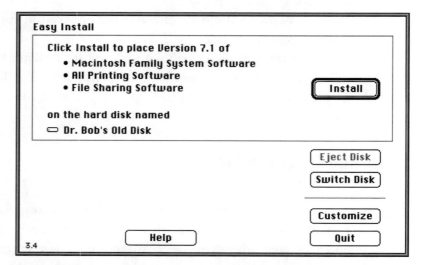

Figure 3.1 The System 7.1 Installer's main installer screen

Install Only What You Need

To do a custom installation, follow these steps:

1 If you are installing the System software on your startup disk (usually your internal hard disk), start your Macintosh with the first Install disk in the drive. On System 7 installation disks, this will automatically launch the Installer. If you are installing another system version, simply insert the first Install disk, double-click its icon if necessary to open it, and double-click the Installer icon to launch the Installer. If you're installing System 6, you may have to double-click the disk icon to open it and double-click the Installer icon to launch the Installer.

2 A "Welcome to the Apple Installer" screen appears. Click **OK**.

3 The **Easy Install** window, which is illustrated in Figure 3.1, appears. Click **Customize**.

4 The **Custom Install** window, which is illustrated in Figure 3.2, appears. Scroll down the list to find the components you need to install. For example, say you have a Macintosh IIcx and a StyleWriter printer and you're not interested in networking software. Scroll down in the list until you find **Software for Style-Writer** and click on it to select it. Its information appears

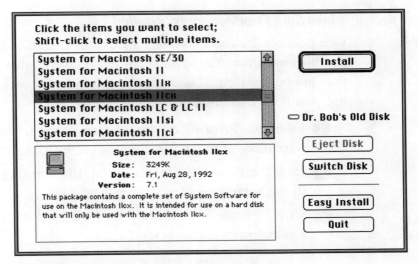

Figure 3.2 Performing a Custom Install

below the scrolling window. Continue to scroll down until you find **System for Macintosh IIcx**. Hold down the **Shift** key and click on it. The list under the scrolling window changes to a list of the software you've selected. You can select whatever options you need from the scrolling list. Just be sure to hold down **Shift** while selecting each one. When you're finished, click **Install**.

5 The installation process begins. Your Macintosh will prompt you to insert disks. Follow the instructions that appear on the screen.

6 When installation is completed, a message appears, telling you that it was successful. Click **Quit** (or **Restart**).

Don't Choose Min System

When doing a **Custom Install**, the Installer's scrolling window of options includes some for **Min System**. If you are installing System software on your startup disk, don't use these options! They create smaller System files that may exclude resources some programs need. They also omit desk accessories and control panels.

Make Sure PrintMonitor Is Installed

One possible drawback to doing a **Custom Install** and not choosing the **Software for All Apple Printers** option is that PrintMonitor may not be installed. If you use PrintMonitor for background printing, you'll have to install it manually.

1 Insert the **Printing** disk that is part of the set of System software disks. If necessary, double-click its icon to open it.

2 Drag the **PrintMonitor** icon from the **Printing** disk window to the **System Folder** on your hard disk.

3 Under System 7, your Macintosh will offer to place it in the **Extensions** folder. Click **OK**.

Install the System Update 3.0

The Macintosh System Update 3.0 is a two-disk set of software "enhancements" that can improve the performance and reliability of Macintosh models running System 7.1, 7.1.1 (System 7 Pro) or 7.1.2 (for the Power Macintosh). It is available for free (or for the cost of a disk) from Apple dealers, some online services, and many Macintosh user groups.

System Update 3.0 consists of a wide variety of System enhancements and bug fixes—far too many to list here. The enhancements improve the way the System works by adding features, like the ability to display color icons in standard Open and Save As dialog boxes. The bug fixes fix System problems that have been discovered since the release of the software.

System Update 3.0 also contains updates to many control panels, desk accessories, and System Enablers used by certain Macintosh models. It also includes updates to utility programs that ship with Macintosh computers:

- ◆ Apple HD SC Setup 7.3.1
- ◆ Disk First Aid 7.2
- ◆ SimpleText 1.0 (which replaces TeachText)

Reinstall the System Software

When reinstalling System software on a disk that already contains a System folder, it's a good idea to start from scratch. There are two good reasons for this:

- ◆ The System Software Installer tends to update existing System files. If your System or Finder are corrupted, the corruption may remain in the updated files.
- ◆ The System Software Installer may delete non-Apple fonts, extensions, and control panels that you need. Replacing them from original disks can be very time consuming.

Follow these steps to reinstall System software on a disk that already has a System file.

1 Start your Macintosh with a bootable floppy. The **Disk Tools** disk that comes with the System software is a good choice. *Don't* start with the first **Install** disk because it may not include a Finder file.

2 Open the **System Folder** on the disk you are reinstalling on (not the floppy disk you started from).

3 Drag the **Finder** file to the **Trash**.

4 If you're running System 7.0.x, double-click the **System** file icon to open it and drag all the non-Apple fonts, sounds, and keyboard layouts out. You may want to put them into a separate folder so they're all together. If you're running System 7.1.x, double-click the **System** file to open it and drag all the non-Apple sounds and keyboard layouts out. If you're running System 6.0.x, use **Font/DA Mover** to copy all non-Apple fonts and desk accessories to one or more suitcase files.

5 Drag the **System** file to the **Trash** and choose **Empty Trash** from the **Special** menu.

6 Rename the **System Folder** to something else, like "Old System Stuff."

7 Follow the instructions in *Install Only What You Need* above to install the System software. Restart your Macintosh.

8 If you're running System 7, open the old System Folder and drag the non-Apple Extensions, Control Panels, Fonts, and Desk Accessories onto your new System Folder icon. Don't drag the folders containing these items—drag the items themselves so your Macintosh puts them away properly and doesn't overwrite existing folders. Open your old Preferences folder and drag its contents onto your new Preferences folder. If you're running System 6, open the old System Folder and drag non-Apple initialization devices and control panels onto your new System Folder. Use Font/DA Mover to reinstall non-Apple fonts and desk accessories. Copy any preferences files in your old System folder to your new one.

9 Drag the old System Folder to the Trash and choose **Empty Trash** from the **Special** menu.

Use this method to reinstall System software whether you're doing an upgrade or reinstalling because of corrupt files.

Run the Compatibility Checker

If you're upgrading from System 6 to System 7 (what took you so long?), run the **Compatibility Checker** that comes with the System software disks. This program analyzes your System 6 system to make sure all your software is compatible with System 7. It creates a report of its results and may move incompatible items out of your System folder into another folder. If all your application software is up to date, however, you shouldn't find any major conflicts with System 7. If you don't have the **Compatibility Checker**, get it from your Apple dealer or look for it on online services or BBSes.

Install the System Software on Another Disk

You can install the System software on a disk other than your startup disk by clicking the **Switch Disk** option in the **Easy Install** or **Custom Install** window (see Figures 3.1 and 3.2) until the name of the disk you want to install on appears.

Deinstall Part of the System Software

The System Software Installer has a **Remove** option hidden away in the **Custom Install** window. Select the component of the System software you want to remove (like a printer driver) and hold down the **Option** key. The **Install** button changes to a **Remove** button, as illustrated in Figure 3.3. Click that button to remove the component from the System Folder on the selected disk. Note that this will only remove certain components from your System.

Create a System 7 Bootable Floppy

System 7 is big, but not too big to fit on a high-density floppy. You can create a System 7 install disk two ways:

♦ Duplicate the **Disk Tools** disk and remove the applications you don't need (like Disk First Aid and Apple HD SC Setup). In System 7.1, that'll leave you with about 220 K of disk space you can use for applications. If you want another 369 K of disk space,

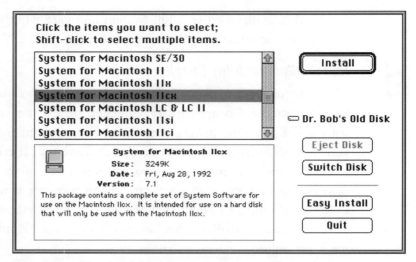

Click the items you want to select;
Shift-click to select multiple items.

System for Macintosh SE/30
System for Macintosh II
System for Macintosh IIx
System for Macintosh IIcx
System for Macintosh LC & LC II
System for Macintosh IIsi
System for Macintosh IIci

Install

Dr. Bob's Old Disk

Eject Disk

Switch Disk

Easy Install

Quit

System for Macintosh IIcx
Size: 3249K
Date: Fri, Aug 28, 1992
Version: 7.1
This package contains a complete set of System Software for use on the Macintosh IIcx. It is intended for use on a hard disk that will only be used with the Macintosh IIcx.

Figure 3.3 The Remove button appears when you hold down the Option key.

delete the Finder. Just remember that you must have an application on a disk in order to start from it. If you delete the Finder and replace it with another application, that application will launch when you boot from the floppy. You will not be able to quit to the Finder.

♦ To create a custom bootable disk that will only work on a certain Macintosh model, you'll need to be able to create a System file without overwriting the one on your Startup disk. That means you need either two floppy disk drives or a spare, non-startup hard disk or removable media. Follow the instructions in Install Only What You Need above to install the **Min System** for the specific computer on this disk. The resulting System folder should fit on a high density floppy disk.

Startup Tricks

The Macintosh startup process begins with a friendly sound, features a parade of icons across the bottom of your screen, and ends with the display of the Finder on your desktop. You might not realize it, but you can control this process. This section tells you how.

Disable System Extensions

The parade of icons across the bottom of your screen at startup indicates that certain installed extensions and control panels are being loaded. System 7 users can easily prevent all of these programs from being loaded by holding down the **Shift** key on startup. When the "Welcome to Macintosh" startup screen appears, they'll see the added message: "Extensions off." This disables all System extensions, control panels, and startup items.

If you're a System 6 user, you must manually remove all initialization devices (the old name for extensions) and control panels before restarting your Macintosh to disable them.

Specify Extension Loading Order

You can specify the loading order of system extensions and control panels two different ways:

♦ Change the name of the extension or control panel so that it comes before or after others alphabetically. In the "File Naming Tricks" section of Chapter 2, you'll find some ideas for getting files to the beginning or end of the list.

♦ System 7 users can also force one control panel to load before the others by simply moving it into the Extensions folder. (The contents of the Extensions folder are loaded first.) Or, load one extension after the others by moving it into the Control Panels folder. Or, load any extension or control panel after all the others by moving it into the System folder (extensions and control panels found there are loaded last).

Customize the Startup Screen

You can change the standard "Welcome to Macintosh" screen to almost anything you like. To do it, you'll need a program that can save graphics files in StartupScreen format, like Kevin Mitchell's *GIFConverter* (shareware), Thorsten Lemke's *GraphicConverter* (shareware), or Aldus Corporation's *SuperPaint*.

Extension Management Software

Although extensions and control panels add all kinds of features—both useful and frivolous, depending on the program—to your Macintosh, they can also cause problems:

- INIT conflicts can occur when two (or more) of these files try to tell your Macintosh to do two things at the same time when your Macintosh simply can't do it. System bombs and unusual behavior result.
- These files expand the size of the system heap, taking up valuable RAM so less is available for your applications.
- Some of these files tell your Macintosh to do so much work in the background that your Macintosh's overall performance drops and operations become very sluggish.

While some extensions and control panels are absolutely necessary for your everyday work, others aren't. If you have more than one full row of icons parading across the bottom of your screen, chances are you should consider removing the ones you can do without.

Another option is to use an extension manager software product. Some good ones include Ricardo Batista/Apple Computer, Inc.'s *Extensions Manager* (freeware) , Now Software Inc.'s *Startup Manager* (part of *Now Utilities*), and Inline Design's *INITPicker*.

1 Use a graphics program that can save in StartupScreen format to create or open a graphic that you'd like to see on your Macintosh screen when you start up.

2 Choose **Save As** from the **File** menu. Save the file in Startup-Screen format—a menu or radio button should give you this option. Name the file "StartupScreen" (without quotes, of course) and save it into the System folder.

When you restart your Macintosh, your startup screen graphic will replace the "Welcome to Macintosh" box.

Use the Startup Items Folder

On a System 7 Macintosh, anything placed in the Startup Items folder inside the System Folder is automatically opened on startup. Here are some ideas for taking advantage of this feature.

♦ To automatically launch an application on startup (like a calendar program or a word processor that you always use), put an alias of that application icon in the Startup Items folder.

♦ To automatically open a document on startup (like your calendar file, an address, book, or perhaps a Things to Do document), put an alias of that document icon in the Startup Items folder.

♦ To automatically play a sound at startup, put a System 7 sound file (or an alias of one) in the Startup Items folder.

You can have as many items as you like in the Startup Items folder. All items will be opened in alphabetical order. When the dust settles, the last opened application or document will display the active window.

Font Tricks

One of the things that set the Macintosh apart from other computers years ago was its ability to use multiple fonts or typefaces in documents. Macintosh users take this for granted now and often collect and install dozens of fonts in their Systems. Here are a few tricks for using and managing your fonts.

Use TrueType Fonts or ATM (or Both)

If font characters appear jagged on screen at certain sizes, you're missing out on the benefits of two font technology gems: TrueType fonts and *Adobe Type Manager* (*ATM*).

TrueType, which is incorporated into System 7 and can be added, with the use of an INIT to System 6.0.7 or 6.0.8, is an Apple Computer font technology. It makes it possible to smoothly scale any TrueType format font to virtually any size on screen or on paper. TrueType fonts come with the Apple System software. Other TrueType fonts are available from many font vendors.

Which Font Is Used on Screen? With bitmapped, TrueType, and PostScript fonts installed in your Macintosh, you may wonder which font is actually used to display characters on screen. Your Macintosh looks for fonts for screen display in the following order:

- Bitmapped in required size
- TrueType
- PostScript (processed with *ATM* if *ATM* is installed)
- Bitmapped (scaled)

ATM is a utility by Adobe Systems Incorporated. It makes it possible to smoothly scale any PostScript Type 1 font to virtually any size on screen or on paper. *ATM* is a "must-have" utility for anyone who uses PostScript fonts and does not have a corresponding TrueType version of the font installed. If you don't have PostScript fonts, however, you don't need *ATM*.

Find and Use Special Characters

Most fonts include more characters than just the letters, numbers, and punctuation marks you see on the keyboard. The characters you don't see—the special characters—can be typed right from your keyboard if you know the proper keystrokes.

Apple gives you a desk accessory you can use to identify all the characters in a font: Key Caps. It's illustrated in Figure 3.4. Here's how you can use it.

1 Choose a font from the **Key Caps** menu. The tops of the keys on your screen change to that font.

2 Press **Shift** to see uppercase characters and regular symbols. (If **Caps Lock** is turned on, you'll see uppercase characters, but you won't see regular symbols unless you press **Shift**.)

3 Press **Option** to see some of the special characters. Note their positions on the keyboard illustration—pressing that character

Figure 3.4 Key Caps displays special characters with the Option key held down.

with the **Option** key held down produces that character. For example, the bullet character (which is available in most fonts) appears at the 8 position. Pressing **Option-8** produces a bullet in most fonts. (Characters that appear as boxes are undefined and shouldn't be used in that font.)

4 Press **Option-Shift** to see some more special characters. These work the same way as the Option characters, but you must press **Option** and **Shift** together while you press a keyboard key to get the special character.

5 You can type characters right into the Key Caps edit box if you like. Or, if you prefer, you can click on the characters you want to use to put them into the edit box.

6 You can select the contents of the Key Caps edit box and copy them to the Clipboard with the **Copy** (**Command-C**) command under the **Edit** menu. You can then paste them into any document with the **Paste** (**Command-V**) command under the Edit menu.

Once you know the keystrokes for the characters you want to use, you don't need Key Caps. Just type the characters right into your documents using the appropriate keystrokes.

Type Accented Characters

Your Macintosh also lets you type accented characters, such as é, ä, ñ, and î. This is a two-step process. The first step tells your Macintosh

A Great Utility for Special Characters

Although Key Caps works, it doesn't have any bells or whistles that make it stand out from other programs. Günther Blascheck's *PopChar*, however, does. This freeware control panel puts a hot spot in your menu bar. Press your mouse button down on this spot and a display of all available characters in the current font appears. Click on a character to insert it into your document instantly. No fooling with desk accessories, no remembering keystrokes. Best of all, this little shareware program is free.

which accent character you want. The second step tells it which character to put under the accent.

Here's a list of the keystrokes to get the accented characters:

Accent Character	Keystroke
`	Option-`
´	Option-E
¨	Option-U
^	Option-I
~	Option-N

So, to type é, press **Option-E** and then **E** by itself. To type ä, press **Option-U** and then **A** by itself. Get the idea? Give it a try. Just remember that not all accented characters are available in all fonts. Your best bets are Times, Helvetica, and Courier.

Remove Seldom-Used Fonts

Fonts take up disk space, increase the size of your System heap, and make **Font** menus long. Remove fonts you don't use to make your System slimmer and trimmer.

Font Utility Software

If you've got lots of fonts installed in your system, you may be interested in a few utilities that can help you manage and use them.

- Fifth Generation Systems' *Suitcase* and AlSoft Inc.'s *MasterJuggler* (part of *ALSoft Power Utilities*) let you store fonts outside your System file or System folder. This makes it possible to quickly and easily install those fonts you need just when you need them.

- Adobe Systems Incorporated's *ATM* was mentioned earlier in this chapter. It's a PostScript interpreter for your Macintosh that can scale PostScript fonts to any size on screen. This eliminates the jagged characters that may appear when your Macintosh tries to scale bitmapped fonts. *SuperATM* can also substitute standard fonts for missing fonts in a document and includes *Adobe Type Reunion* to group font families in menus.

- Now Software, Inc.'s *WYSIWYG Menus* (part of *Now Utilities*) displays fonts in their actual typefaces in application Font menus.

Monitor Tricks

If you've got a Macintosh with a color monitor, you'll see that it can do tricks, too.

Reduce Colors to Increase Speed

The more colors (or shades of gray) your Macintosh monitor needs to display, the harder it needs to work to display them. You can often speed up your Macintosh simply by reducing the number of colors it displays.

1 Open the **Monitors** control panel. The color depth options offered in the scrolling window at the top of the control panel will vary depending on your system's color capabilities. (See Figure 3.5.) If your system supports 8-bit color, the maximum will be 256 colors. If it supports 32-bit color, the maximum will be billions of colors.

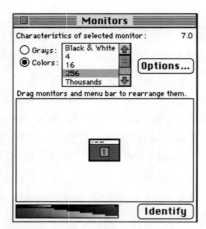

Figure 3.5 The Monitors
control panel lets you
change color depth.

2 Click one of the options for fewer colors than your system can
support. You might want to try 4 or 16. If your system can
support thousands or millions of colors, try 256 colors. If you
want a radical change, try Black and White.

Keep in mind that some graphics programs and games require a certain color depth. If that's the case, you'll have to reopen the **Monitors**
control panel and change the color depth back to at least the minimum
required for that program before using it.

Working with Multiple Monitors

If you've got more than one monitor connected to your Macintosh, you
can set them up so that you can use both at the same time.

1 Open the **Monitors** Control Panel. The monitor arrangement
appears at the bottom of the control panel window. (See Figure 3.6.)

2 Drag either monitor icon to position it beside, above, or below
the other.

3 If desired, drag the menu bar from one monitor to the other.
The monitor with the menu bar becomes the primary monitor.

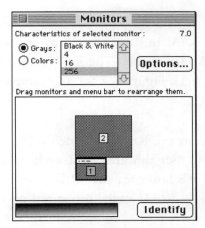

Figure 3.6 **Setting up two monitors**

4 You can also set the color depth for each monitor. Click on one of the monitor icons in the control panel to select it, then change the color depth at the top of the control panel. They don't have to be the same.

You may have to restart your Macintosh for changes to take effect. Once you've set this up, you'll find that your mouse can move off one monitor and onto the other. You can place document windows on either monitor.

See a Happy Mac

To see a happy Mac, open the **Monitors** control panel and hold down the **Option** key.

RAM Tricks

. . . .

RAM, like disk space, is another computer component there never seems to be enough of. Fortunately, many Macintosh models can accept lots of RAM—up to 256 MB in some models. This section offers some tips and tricks for using the RAM you have and getting more RAM when you need it—all without opening your Macintosh.

Examine RAM Usage

Check the amount of RAM in use and free by choosing **About This Macintosh** from the **Apple** menu. (The Finder must be the active application to do this.) Check Figure 3.7 for an example.

Use the Cache

A disk cache is a special area of RAM set aside for frequently used information. Your Macintosh uses this area to store instructions it thinks it might use again. Since it's faster for the CPU to get instructions from RAM than the hard disk, a RAM cache can speed up your Macintosh's operations.

System 7 users can set the **Disk Cache** with the **Memory** control panel, which is illustrated in Figure 3.8. System 6 users can set the **Cache** in the **General** control panel. Use the arrows to increase or decrease the setting. Keep in mind that the larger you make the cache, the larger your System heap will be. This decreases the amount of RAM available for applications.

Don't Set the Cache Too High!

If the disk cache can speed up your Macintosh by giving it a place to store and retrieve frequently used instructions, the bigger the disk cache, the faster your Macintosh should run, right? Wrong. The CPU searches the cache for needed instructions before it looks on your hard disk. If the cache is very large, it spends a lot of time searching for instructions that may or may not be there. After a certain point, this can actually slow down your Macintosh. Most hardware gurus recommend setting the cache to 32 K per 1 MB of RAM. That means about 256 K for an 8 MB Macintosh.

In addition to all this, some graphics programs have their own recommended cache settings. Consult the documentation for the applications you use most to see what they recommend. Then set your cache at a level that should be acceptable to all of them.

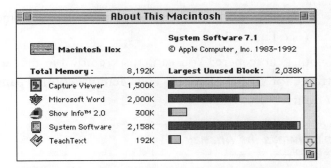

Figure 3.7 About This Macintosh shows RAM usage.

Use Virtual Memory to Add RAM for Free

If you see the "Not Enough Memory..." message too often on your Macintosh and aren't ready to invest hard cash on additional RAM, virtual memory might be the answer. Virtual memory fools your Macintosh into thinking that an invisible file it creates on disk is really RAM. You turn on virtual memory with the Memory control panel.

1 Open the **Memory** control panel.

2 Choose the **On** radio button in the **Virtual Memory** area.

3 Use the **Hard Disk** pop-up menu to choose a hard disk. The amount of hard disk space and real RAM will determine the amount of virtual memory you can create. Use the arrows that

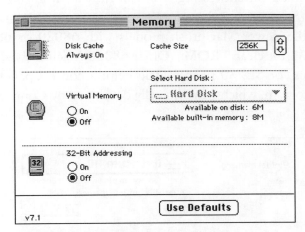

Figure 3.8 The Memory control panel

appear to select the total amount of virtual memory you want. (See Figure 3.9.)

A quick note here: You can't use removable media like a SyQuest cartridge for virtual memory. The Memory control panel just won't let you do it.

Virtual Memory Isn't Always the Answer

When using virtual memory, there are two important things to keep in mind:

♦ Virtual memory is slower than real RAM. This can slow down your Macintosh. Because of this, it's not a good idea to depend on virtual memory to meet long-term RAM needs.

♦ Virtual memory uses up hard disk space. The invisible file it creates on disk will be equal to the total RAM you end up with. So if you've got 13 MB of virtual memory, that's 13 MB of hard disk space you can't use for file storage.

Get Beyond the 8 MB RAM Barrier

If you want to install more than 8 MB of RAM in your Macintosh, you'll have to turn on 32-bit addressing to use it. If your Macintosh supports 32-bit addressing, you can turn it on in the Memory control panel. (See Figure 3.8.)

All the newer Macintosh models with 68030 or 68040 processors have "32-bit clean" ROMs. Older 68030 Macintoshes, like the Mac II, IIx, IIcx, or SE/30 need a little help: a control panel called *Mode32*. This program, which was originally developed by Connectix Corporation,

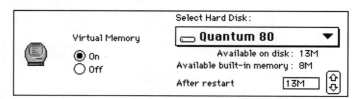

Figure 3.9 A closer look at Virtual Memory settings

RAMDoubler and Other RAM Software
If you want more RAM but don't want to buy and install RAM chips, check out Connectix Corporation's *RAMDoubler*. This program can double the amount of installed RAM on your Macintosh. Connectix makes a number of other RAM-related software products, too.

was licensed by Apple Computer, Inc. and is freely distributable. You can find it on many online services and BBSes.

Create and Use a RAM Disk

A RAM disk is the opposite of virtual memory. When you create a RAM disk, you're using RAM as disk storage space. When used properly, it can reduce the number of times your Macintosh accesses its hard disk. This is especially useful for PowerBook users who need to extend battery life.

About RAM Fragmentation
In order to launch an application, you must have enough free contiguous RAM to meet its RAM allocation needs. For example, to open a program that requires 1024 K of RAM, you must have that much contiguous space. You can see how much contiguous RAM is available in the **About This Macintosh** window beside **Largest Unused Block**. (See Figures 3.7 and 3.10.)

As you work with your Macintosh, opening and closing applications throughout the day, RAM gets fragmented. This is a normal occurrence and has no side effects other than reducing contiguous RAM. You can tell if RAM has been fragmented by consulting the **About This Macintosh** window. If the total RAM used by applications plus the **Largest Unused Block** does not equal the **Total Memory**, your RAM is fragmented. This is illustrated in Figure 3.10, where the total RAM used is 7017 K, the **Total Memory** is 8192 K, and the **Largest Free Block** is only 622 K. The missing 553 K of RAM is not part of the **Largest Free Block** and cannot be used.

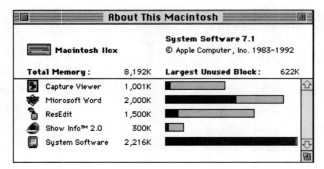

Figure 3.10 When the numbers don't add up,
RAM is fragmented.

Apple provides a RAM disk utility with PowerBooks. If you don't like Apple's utility, check out Connectix Corporation's *Maxima* and Mark Adams' *AppDisk* (shareware). AppDisk is especially useful because it's an application and doesn't require you to restart your Macintosh to use it. With it, you can create and remove a RAM disk on the fly.

RAM Disk Danger

Even when RAM is used as a disk, it's still RAM. That means that if your Macintosh shuts down because of a System bomb, power outage, or you choose the Shut Down or Restart commands, everything on the RAM disk will be lost. A good RAM disk utility will automatically copy the contents of the RAM disk to real disk space periodically. Be sure the contents of your RAM disk are copied to real disk before you shut down your Macintosh.

Defragment RAM

There are two ways to defragment RAM:

♦ Quit all open applications. Often, this is enough to restore the **Largest Free Block** to its maximum size.

♦ Restart your Macintosh to completely clear RAM and start fresh. This is a foolproof way to maximize the **Largest Free Block**.

Map Tricks

• •

Many people think that the Map control panel is nothing more than a cute map of the world. It does have a practical use, however: You can use it to localize your Macintosh. Here are some tricks for using and customizing the Map.

Tell Your Macintosh Where It Is

By localizing your Macintosh, you tell it where it is. While this might not be important for desktop Macintosh models, it's useful for Power-Books. Localizing your Macintosh automatically adjusts the system clock.

1 In the Map control panel (illustrated in Figure 3.11), type in the name of the closest major city and click **Find**.

2 If it finds the city you've entered, an asterisk blinks there on the map. Click **Set** to select that as the current location. If it doesn't find the city, read on to learn how you can add a city and view all cities.

Find Out Distances Between Two Cities

When you use the **Find** button to find a city, the Map control panel automatically displays the distance between that city and the "set" city as well as the local time in the found city.

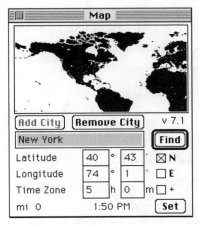

Figure 3.11 **The Map control panel**

Add a City to the Map

If your city isn't one of those programmed into the map, you can add it.

1 In the Map control panel type in the name of the city, its **Longitude**, its **Latitude**, and the number of hours its time is before or after Greenwich mean time. Use the **N** and **E** check boxes to specify locations north of the equator or east of Greenwich. Use the **+** check box to specify whether the hours in the time zone difference should be added to or subtracted from Greenwich mean time. If you don't know a city's longitude and latitude, you can click on the map to indicate its approximate location.

2 Click **Add City** to add the city to the list of cities on the map.

Scroll Through All Map Locations

If you're curious to see what cities are included on the Map, hold down the **Option** key and press **Return** to cycle through all of them in alphabetical order, beginning with the last one you found. The map view changes to show each city.

Zoom In to the Map

To zoom in on the map view, hold down the **Option** key while opening the Map control panel.

Colorize the Map

If you have a color monitor and would like to replace the boring black and white map with something a little more interesting, follow these steps:

1 Open the Scrapbook desk accessory.

2 Scroll through the images until you find the one with the color map.

3 Choose **Copy** (**Command-C**) from the **Edit** menu.

4 Close the Scrapbook.

5 Open the **Map** control panel.

6 Choose **Paste** (**Command-V**) from the **Edit** menu.

7 A dialog box with the following message appears: "Paste will replace the current map with the picture in the Clipboard. Are you sure you want to do this?" Click **Replace**.

The color map image replaces the standard one.

Find the Middle of Nowhere

If you've ever wondered where the middle of nowhere is, use the Map control panel to find it.

Miscellaneous System Tricks

Here are a few tricks that couldn't be categorized elsewhere in this chapter. You might find them useful.

Customize Your Keyboard

The Keyboard control panel, which is illustrated in Figure 3.12, lets you customize the way your keyboard works.

♦ Click a radio button to choose a **Key Repeat Rate**. This specifies how quickly a key should repeat when you hold that key down.

♦ Click a radio button to choose the **Delay Until Repeat**. This specifies how long your Macintosh waits before it starts repeating a key you hold down.

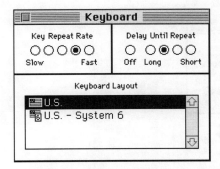

Figure 3.12 The Keyboard control panel

Switch Keyboard Layouts

System 7 users can install additional keyboard layouts by dragging them onto the System file icon. This can be very handy if you often have to type in foreign languages or if you prefer a Dvorak keyboard layout for faster typing. Keyboard layouts are often available from font vendors and on online services and BBSes.

If you have more than one keyboard layout installed in your System file, you can switch among them depending on your needs. There are two ways to do this:

♦ Open the Keyboard control panel (see Figure 3.12), choose the one you want from the scrolling list, and close the Keyboard control panel.

♦ Press **Command-Option-Spacebar** to select the next layout alphabetically without opening the Keyboard control panel.

Customize Your Mouse

The Mouse control panel, which is illustrated in Figure 3.13, lets you customize the way your mouse works.

♦ Click a radio button to choose a **Mouse Tracking** speed. This changes the speed the mouse moves on screen in relation to the actual mouse movement.

♦ Click a radio button to choose **Double-click Speed**. If you just can't seem to double-click fast enough to satisfy your Macintosh, this is where you can tell it to expect slower double-clicks.

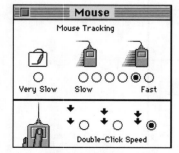

Figure 3.13 The Mouse control panel

Maintain More Than One System Folder

If you find yourself needing to switch back and forth between two versions of the System software—perhaps System 6 and System 7—having two System folders can help. Although it is *not* a good idea to have both System folders on the same disk (your Macintosh can get confused and look at the wrong files), there's no reason why you can't have one on your internal hard disk and another one on an external hard disk or removable media.

To do this, use Apple's System Software Installer to install a second System Folder on another disk. To switch from one to the other, do this:

♦ With System 7 running, use the **Startup Disk** control panel, which is illustrated in Figure 3.14, to choose a disk you want your Macintosh to boot from when you restart. Then restart.

♦ With System 6 running, open the **Control Panel** desk accessory and choose the **Startup Device** icon. Then choose the disk you want to boot from. Close the **Control Panel** and restart.

If you do this a lot, you may want to check into a handy freeware program called *Switcher* by Keisuke Hara. It automatically searches for all mounted disks that contain System Folders and lets you pick the disk to boot from. If you pick a System 6 System Folder, it even lets you choose between Finder and MultiFinder.

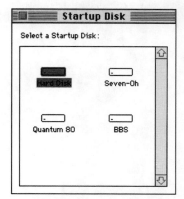

Figure 3.14 The Startup
Disk control panel

One thing to keep in mind here: When you switch from System 6 to System 7, your Macintosh will rebuild its Desktop file automatically. Don't stop it; it needs to update this information. You'll then have two versions of this invisible file on your disk. In Chapter 10, you'll see how you can delete one of them.

Try a System Optimizer

Several shareware products can "optimize" your System, adding keyboard shortcuts, changing the way things work to speed them up, and letting you customize the appearance of your Macintosh. Among these are *Speedy Finder 7* by Victor Tan, *System 7 Pack!* and *System 7 Companion Pack!* by Adam Stein, and *FinderEdit* by Dan Weisman. Look for these products on online services and BBSes.

Chapter 4

· ·

Software Tricks

A computer is completely useless without software. Macintosh users depend on applications like Microsoft Word, Claris MacWrite Pro, Claris FileMaker Pro, ClarisWorks, Microsoft Excel, QuarkXPress, and Aldus PageMaker to create documents and get their work done.

In this chapter, you'll find some tricks for installing, launching, and using applications. Although most of the tricks in this chapter will work with any application, you'll find a few application-specific tricks as well. For even more tricks for your favorite applications, check out the rest of the *Slick Trick* series of books.

Installation Tricks

· ·

Before you can use software, you need to install it. In the old days, most programs came on just one floppy disk. You'd drag the program icons from the disk window to your hard disk and get to work. Nowadays, many programs come on multiple disks and have fancy installers like— Apple's System Software Installer—that let you decide what to install.

How do you decide? How can you install software quickly and easily? That's what this section is about.

Read the Read Me File

The first installation disk for many programs includes a "Read Me" file. This file, which is normally in plain text or TeachText-readable format, provides important information about installation and program features that is not included in the software or installation manuals. Read this file *before* you install the software. It could contain installation instructions you'll need to install it right on the first try.

Install Only What You Need

When a program comes on seven high-density floppy disks, you can bet it's going to take up a lot of space on your hard disk when you install it. But it doesn't have to be that way. Like Apple's System Software Installer, most installers let you choose what to install. (In fact, many installers are based on Apple's Installer so they look and work the same way. Check Chapter 3 for details on Apple's Installer.) Figure 4.1 shows an example of the main installer screen for Microsoft Excel 4.0. Notice how it offers **Complete**, **Custom**, **Minimum**, and **Network** installation options. If you click **Custom**, the installer offers check boxes to choose components of the program. You can see this in Figure 4.2.

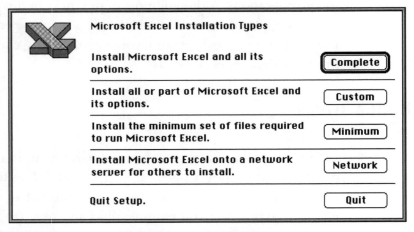

Figure 4.1 Microsoft Excel's main installer screen

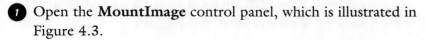

```
Select Options, Disk and Folder:
                                    [🗀 Applications ▼]
⊠ Microsoft Excel          1890K    🗀 ClarisWorks    ⬆   ⊂ Dr. Bob'...
   ⊠ Spelling Checker       420K    🗀 FileMaker Pro
⊠ Macro Library            981K    🗀 Word                  [  Eject   ]
⊠ Microsoft Excel Help    1661K
⊠ Microsoft Excel Tutorial 1554K                           [ Desktop  ]
⊠ Dialog Editor             45K
⊠ Example Files            125K                            [   Open   ]
⊠ Microsoft Analysis ToolPak 950K
⊠ Microsoft Excel Solver   303K                           [  Setup   ]
⊠ Crosstab ReportWizard    632K
⊠ Data Access              174K                            [   Quit   ]
   ⊠ Autostart               3K    ⬇
                                                           [New Folder]
      Total Space Required:   8736K
         Space Available:    47616K
      Installation folder: Applications
```

Figure 4.2 Microsoft Excel's custom install screen

Not all installers work the same way, but if you need to install software, always check the custom installation options first. You can save disk space and reduce the amount of RAM a program requires to run by installing only the features and components you need.

Install Other Components Later

If you've installed an application with **Custom** or **Minimum** installation options, you may find later that certain features you need are missing. In most cases, you can use the software's installer to simply add the missing features, rather than reinstalling all the software from scratch. This can save a lot of time and disk swapping.

Use Disk Images to Install Software Without Swapping Disks

If the software you need to install is in disk image files, you can often install it without swapping disks at all. To do this, you need a disk image mounting utility. *MountImage* by Steve Christensen is a freely distributable control panel that you can find on many online services and BBSes.

1 Open the **MountImage** control panel, which is illustrated in Figure 4.3.

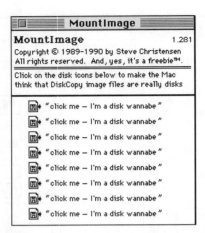

Figure 4.3 The *MountImage*
control panel

2 Click an icon beside the words "click me—I'm a disk wannabe."

3 Use the standard **Open** dialog box that appears to locate and **Open** a disk image file. A floppy disk icon appears on your Desktop.

4 Repeat Steps 2 and 3 for each disk you want on your Desktop. You can open up to eight disk images this way. Your Macintosh thinks each icon that appears on your Desktop is a real floppy disk, no matter how many floppy disk drives your Macintosh has.

5 Close *MountImage*.

MountImage and Mt.Image

System 7 users can mount disk images with a drag-and-drop interface with *Mt.Image*, a freeware drag-and-drop application by "Basuke." Although it requires that *MountImage* be installed properly in your Control Panels folder, it enables you to bypass *MountImage*'s control panel interface. To mount a disk image file, simply drop its icon onto the *Mt.Image* file icon.

6 If necessary, double-click on the first installer disk's icon to open it. Launch the installer and follow the instructions that appear on your screen to start the installation process. Now go get a cup of coffee or soda while your Macintosh installs the software. You will not be asked to insert any disks.

RAM Allocation Tricks

. . . .

The amount of RAM an application takes up when it's launched is determined by the settings in the **Get Info** window for that application. Chapter 1 looked at this briefly. In this section, you'll learn more about an application's RAM needs.

Find How Much RAM Is Really Used

As discussed in Chapter 3, the **About This Macintosh** window shows RAM usage. For each open application, it displays a bar. The total bar length is determined by the amount of RAM allocated to the program in the **Get Info** window. This is called the application heap. The dark gray portion of the bar represents the amount of RAM actually used by the application at that moment. The light gray portion represents the amount of additional RAM in the application heap that is not in use by the application. Here's how System 7 users can find out exactly how much is in use.

1 With at least one application (other than the Finder) open, choose **About This Macintosh** from the **Apple** menu. (The Finder must be the active application for this option to appear.)

2 Choose **Show Balloons** from the **Help** (or **Balloon Help**) menu.

3 Point to the bar for one of the open applications. The amount of RAM in use is displayed in the balloon, as illustrated in Figure 4.4.

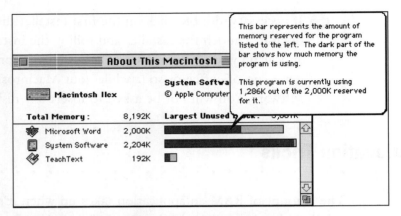

Figure 4.4 Balloon Help has at least one practical use.

Find Out How Much RAM an Application Really Needs

Using the information you get from balloon help in the **About This Macintosh** window, you can determine approximately how much RAM an application needs to run.

1. Launch an application you use often. Use it to open the number and type of documents you normally work with at once.

2. Follow the instructions under "Find How Much RAM Is Really Used" above to find out how much of the application heap the application uses during an average session.

Generally speaking, the application heap bar should always have *some* light gray area. Recommendations on how much of the application heap should remain free range from 5 to 25 percent of the total heap size. In Figure 4.4, Microsoft Word is using only 1286 K of the 2000 K set aside for it. That means nearly 36 percent of the application heap is free. (You can calculate the percentage of free space by taking the difference between the actual amount used and the amount set aside and dividing that by the amount set aside: $(2000-1286)/2000 = .357$.) If the number and type of documents currently open is a good representation of a normal session, the RAM allocation for Word could be reduced to free up RAM for more applications. Of course, if the amount of free space were only 5 percent, the RAM allocation should probably be increased to give the application some "breathing space."

Whatever you decide, keep in mind that additional RAM allocated to an application could make the application run faster. Only through making changes and evaluating results can you get an idea of how the RAM allocation should be set for the best results.

Set the RAM Allocation

Setting the RAM Allocation in the **Get Info** window lets you tell your Macintosh exactly how much RAM to use.

1. If the application is open, choose **Quit** from the **File** menu to quit it.
2. Click once on the application icon to select it.
3. Choose **Get Info** from the **File** menu.

The application's RAM allocation can be set in the bottom of the **Get Info** window. How this area of the **Get Info** window looks depends on the version of the System software you're using, as illustrated in Figure 4.5.

♦ On a System 6.0.x Macintosh, you can only change the RAM allocation when you're using MultiFinder. The **Suggested Memory Size** is what the programmer recommends for the program. The **Application Memory Size** edit box is where you can enter a new value.

♦ On a System 7.0.x Macintosh, the **Suggested Size** is what the programmer recommends for the program. The **Current Size** edit box is where you can enter a new value.

♦ On a System 7.1.x Macintosh, there are three RAM allocation numbers. The **Suggested Size** is what the programmer recommends for the program. The **Minimum Size** edit box is where

Figure 4.5 RAM allocation options for System 6.0.x, System 7.0.x, and System 7.1.x

you can enter a minimum RAM allocation for launching the application when there is a RAM shortage—in this case, your Macintosh will use whatever RAM is available to launch the program, but will never use less than the **Minimum Size** you specify. The **Preferred Size** edit box is where you can enter the amount of RAM you really want the program to use. When you launch the program, your Macintosh will check available RAM and then use whatever it can, up to this value.

Be Careful When Setting Sizes!

 If you enter a value less than the Suggested Size in a RAM Allocation edit box, a warning dialog box like the one in Figure 4.6 may appear when you close the **Get Info** window. Heed this warning! Running an application with less than the RAM recommended by its programmer can cause unreliable program operation and loss of data.

Drag-and-Drop Tricks

System 7 introduced drag-and-drop applications. Simply drag a document file onto an application icon and the document opens with that application (provided the application can open that type of document). Here are some tricks for taking advantage of the drag-and-drop features of System 7.

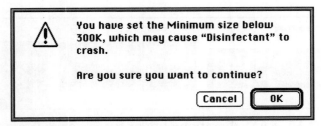

Figure 4.6 A warning you should heed

Open a Document Created by One Application with Another

You can use drag and drop to open a document created by one application with another application—for example, opening a Microsoft Word document with Claris MacWrite Pro. Simply drag the document icon onto the icon for the application you want to open it with and let go. When the outline of the document icon moves on top of the application icon, the application icon becomes highlighted, as illustrated in Figure 4.7. If the application is already running, the document simply opens in that application. If the application not already running, the application launches first, then opens the document.

Drag-and-Drop Notes

There are two things to keep in mind when using drag and drop to open documents:

♦ Not all applications can open all documents. If you drag a document icon onto an application icon and the application icon does not become highlighted, the application will not open that document.

♦ When you save a document, it gets the type and creator code of the application you saved it in. So if you open a Word document with MacWrite Pro and save it, it becomes a MacWrite Pro document.

Open Multiple Documents at Once

You can use drag and drop to open more than one document at a time. Simply drag multiple document icons onto an application icon to open them all.

Figure 4.7 Drag and drop opens a document created by one application with another.

Drag and Drop onto Aliases

If you use drag and drop to open documents on a regular basis, make aliases of your favorite drag and drop applications and either keep them on your Desktop or in a folder on your Desktop. Drag and drop works with aliases as well as original application files.

Template Tricks

A template is a formatted document file that you use to create new documents with similar layouts. Templates can be used as forms for memos, fax transmittal sheets, reports, letters, newsletters, financial reports—almost any kind of document that is created repeatedly with consistent formatting. Templates save time and effort by eliminating the need to format documents.

The trick to creating and using templates is to make sure the original template file is not overwritten by a completed document based on the template. System 7 offers Stationery files just for this purpose. This section tells you how to create templates as well as how to take advantage of templates in some popular Macintosh applications.

Create Templates with Get Info

The **Get Info** window offers two ways to turn a regular document into a template.

1. Create and save a document you want to use as a template.
2. Quit the application that you used to create the document.
3. Locate the document icon and click once on it to select it.
4. Choose **Get Info** (**Command-I**) from the **File** menu.
5. Turn on either the **Locked** check box or the **Stationery pad** check box, as shown in Figure 4.8. The **Locked** check box, which is also available to System 6 users, makes it impossible to save the same file with the same name. The **Stationery pad** check box turns the document into a System 7 Stationery file. Opening a Stationery file automatically opens an Untitled document with the same exact formatting and contents of the

Figure 4.8 The Get Info window offers two options to create templates.

Stationery file. Note that if you turn on **Stationery pad**, the file's icon may change.

6 Click the close box to close the **Get Info** window.

Create Templates with Save As

The **Save As** command in most applications offers an opportunity to save a file as a Stationery file. Opening Stationery automatically opens an Untitled document with the same exact formatting and contents as the Stationery file.

1 Create a document you want to use as a template.

2 Choose **Save As** from the **File** menu.

3 Use the directory portion of the window to open the folder you will save the file into.

4 Enter a name for the file. You might want to include the word "Template" as part of the file name so you can identify it easily in directory dialog boxes.

5 Look for a pull down menu, radio button, or other method to specify that the file should be saved as a **Stationery** file or **Template**. Usually, this option is offered right in the dialog box, as shown in Word's **Save As** dialog box in Figure 4.9. Some programs, like Excel, hide it behind an **Options** or **File Type** button. If you can't find a way to specify that the file should be saved as Stationery, consult the documentation that came with the program. ("When all else fails, check the manual.")

6 Click the **Save** button.

Word Templates in Work Menu

You can have a Microsoft Word template automatically appear in a custom **Work** menu on your menu bar, as shown in Figure 4.10. This makes templates quick and easy to open.

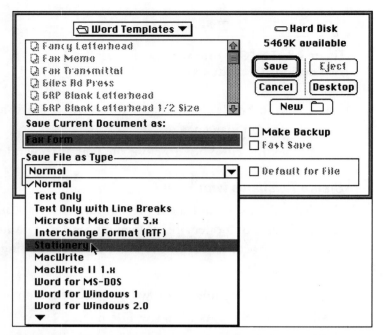

Figure 4.9 The Save As dialog box of Microsoft Word lets you create Stationery files when you save.

① Create the template document with Word.

② Choose **Save As** from the **File** menu.

③ Use the directory portion of the Save As dialog box to open a folder to save the file into. It can be saved in any folder.

④ Choose **Stationery** from the **Save File as Type** pop-up menu.

⑤ Enter a name for the template.

⑥ Click **Save** to save the document.

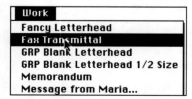

Figure 4.10 Adding Word templates to a Work menu

7 With any Word document active on screen, press **Command-Option-Shift-=**. The mouse pointer turns into a bold plus sign (**+**).

8 Use the plus sign pointer to choose **Open** (**Command-O**) from the **File** menu.

9 Use the **Open** dialog box to locate and **Open** the template document you want on the menu. When you click **Open**, the dialog box closes and the file is listed under the **Work** menu. If you did not already have a **Work** menu, **Word** creates one for you.

Add Excel Templates to New Dialog

You can have a Microsoft Excel template automatically appear in the scrolling list of document types in the **New** dialog box, as shown in Figure 4.11.

1 Create the template document with Excel.

2 Choose **Save As** from the **File** menu.

3 Use the directory portion of the **Save As** dialog box to open the Excel Startup folder inside the Preferences folder inside the System Folder.

4 Click **Options**.

5 Choose **Template** from the **File Format** pop-up menu.

6 Click **OK**.

7 Enter a name for the template.

8 Click **Save**.

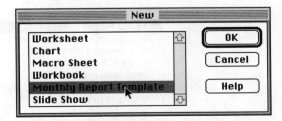

Figure 4.11 Displaying Excel templates in the New dialog box

ClarisWorks Templates in New Document Dialog

You can have a ClarisWorks template automatically appear in the pop-up **Stationery** menu of the **New Document** dialog box, as shown in Figure 4.12. Claris calls this *Easy Stationery*.

1 Create the template document with ClarisWorks.

2 Choose **Save As** from the **File** menu.

3 Use the directory portion of the **Save As** dialog box to open the ClarisWorks Stationery folder inside the Claris folder inside the System Folder.

4 Choose **Stationery** from the **Save As** pop-up menu.

5 Enter a name for the template.

6 Click **Save** to save the document.

Word Processor Tricks

Although word processors have been steadily sending typewriters to the trash heap for at least the past ten years, many Macintosh users continue to "type" with their word processors. What does this mean? Simply that

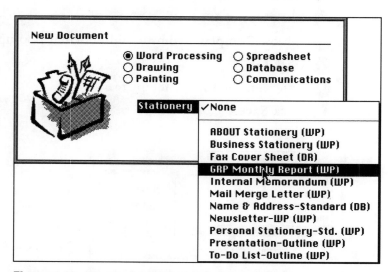

Figure 4.12 Displaying ClarisWorks templates in the New Document dialog box

they are not taking advantage of all the features their word processors have to offer. In this section, you'll find some tips and tricks for getting more out of your word processing application.

View Invisible Characters

Spaces, **Tabs**, and **Returns** are all examples of invisible characters—you can't see them when you print, but they're there. Most word processing applications enable you to view invisible characters on your screen. This can be handy when formatting text. You can see examples of hidden characters in Figures 4.13 through 4.16.

Here's how you can show invisible characters in some popular Word processors:

♦ In Microsoft Word, click the **Show/Hide ¶** button on the Standard toolbar.

♦ In Claris MacWrite Pro, choose **Show Invisibles** (**Command-;**) from the **View** menu. (If **Hide Invisibles** is displayed on the **View** menu, invisible characters are already showing.)

♦ In ClarisWorks, choose **Preferences** from the **Edit** menu. In the **Preferences** dialog box that appears, make sure the **Text** icon is selected and turn on the check box for **Show Invisibles**. Then click **OK**.

Use Tabs Correctly

Most popular word processing applications, like Microsoft Word, Claris MacWrite Pro, and the word processing module of ClarisWorks, have full-featured tab controls. Use them to set tabs to create small tables of information, like the tables you'll find throughout this book. Here are some things to keep in mind:

♦ Word processors offer several types of tabs. Use the appropriate type for the alignment you need. Figure 4.13 illustrates the types of tabs (and the setting markers) you'll find in Word and MacWrite Pro. (ClarisWorks is virtually identical to MacWrite Pro.) Note the similarities. If you use a different word processor, your tab controls may look like these.

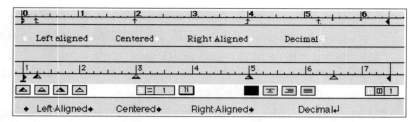

Figure 4.13 Tabs available in two popular word processors

♦ In order to use a tab stop setting, you must press the Tab key on the keyboard to move the insertion point to the tab stop indicator. Then type.

♦ Tabs can be different for every paragraph in a document. Once you set tabs for one paragraph, and you press return at the end of that paragraph, the settings are carried forward to the next. To change the tab settings for multiple paragraphs at the same time, you must select the paragraphs first.

Don't Press Tab Repeatedly or Use the Space Bar!

If you think you can get around setting tabs by simply pressing the tab key repeatedly until your text lines up, don't kid yourself. Doing this—or, what's worse, using the space bar to line up text—may come back to haunt you when you make formatting changes later on. Remember, most Macintosh fonts are proportional: Each character in each font has a different width. Figure 4.14 shows a table in a Word document created by a lazy person. The gray dots, arrows, and backwards P's are Space, Tab, and Return characters, none of which print. Look what happens when the font changes from Times to Helvetica!

Use Indents Correctly

Most word processors also have full-featured indentation settings. Use them to set three different indents: left first line, left (other than first line), and right. Figure 4.15 shows the indent markers and the effect on a short paragraph in Word and MacWrite Pro.

Year(s)◆	◆	Top·Product◆	◆	Top·Salesperson◆	Top·Region¶
1991/1992/1993◆	◆	Ice·Cream◆◆	◆	Janice◆·◆	North·East¶
1994◆·◆	◆	Whoopie·Cushions◆·◆		Mary·Ellen◆	South·Central¶
1995·(estimated)◆	◆	Water·Pistols◆	◆	Don◆·◆	South·America¶
¶					
Year(s)◆◆	◆	Top·Product◆	◆	Top·Salesperson◆·◆	Top·Region¶
1991/1992/1993◆	◆	Ice·Cream◆	◆	Janice◆	◆ ···
North·East¶					
1994◆·◆	◆	Whoopie·Cushions◆	◆	Mary·Ellen◆	South·
Central¶					
1995·(estimated)◆	◆	Water·Pistols◆	◆	◆	Don◆·◆	South·
America¶					

Figure 4.14 **Using multiple tab and space characters can get you into trouble when you reformat.**

Here are some additional tips and tricks for using indents correctly:

♦ To indent the first line of a paragraph, set the left first line indent to the right of the left indent. This is illustrated in Figure 4.15.

♦ To create a "hanging indent" (often used for bulleted or numbered lists), set the left indent to the right of the left first line indent.

♦ Indent settings can be different for every paragraph in a document. Once you set indents for one paragraph, if you press Return at the end of that paragraph, the settings are carried forward to the next. To change indent settings for multiple paragraphs at the same time, you must select the paragraphs first.

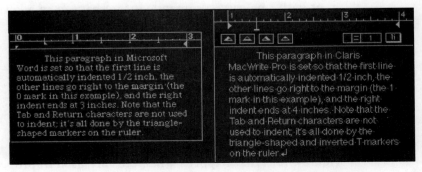

Figure 4.15 Three indent settings in two word processors

Don't Confuse Indents with Tabs... or with Margins!

Indents and tabs are very different. Indents work with the word wrap feature of the word processor to ensure that text lines up properly on the far left and right sides, even after it is edited. Tabs work to line up information in columns. Figure 4.16 shows an example of tabs used improperly for indentation. Look what happens when additional text is inserted into the paragraph!

Indents and margins are also different. While indents determine where text will begin and end on a line, margins determine the overall print area for the page or document. Indents can be different for each paragraph. Margins must be the same for an entire page—and usually for an entire document.

Use Style Sheets

Most word processors offer a **Style** or **Style Sheet** feature. Whenever possible, use this feature to create a number of formats you plan to use throughout your document. Then, when you want to format some text, you can apply the style to the text and see the changes instantly.

Here's an example. Say you're creating a report with headings, numbered lists, and standard or normal text. Each of these components requires different formatting—different fonts, sizes, styles, indentation settings, line spacing, etc. By creating a separate style for each of these components, you can apply all the necessary formatting to the component with one easy command—or perhaps even a keystroke! This saves time and ensures consistent formatting.

```
1)◆    Never·use·tabs·when·indents·would·be·more·appropriate.·This·is·a·good·¶
◆      example·of·how·things·could·get·messed·up!¶
¶
1)◆    Never·use·tabs·when·indents·would·be·more·appropriate.·When·you·insert·or·
delete·text·word·wrap·changes.·This·is·a·good¶
◆      example·of·how·things·could·get·messed·up!¶
```

Figure 4.16 What happens when tabs are used improperly for indentation

Here are some additional things to consider when working with styles:

♦ Word processors provide paragraph style (for entire paragraphs), character style (for selected characters), or both. If you're not sure which one your Word processor supports, check the manual that came with it.

♦ You can override an applied style by either applying another style or simply selecting text and making formatting changes to it.

♦ If you change the definition for a style, all the text in your document that uses that style will change accordingly. This is perhaps the best advantage of using of styles.

♦ Styles can be incorporated into Template documents. They can often also be copied from one document to another in the same application.

♦ Styles created in one program can often be read by another. For example, QuarkXPress, a popular page layout program, can read styles from a Word document.

 ### Use Find and Replace to Save Keystrokes

You've created a 12-page report that refers over and over to "XYZ Company." Well, this week XYZ Company changed its name to ABC Company. What do you do? Use the Find and Replace (or just plain Replace) feature of your word processor to search for the old text and replace it with new text. Most word processors let you replace occurrences one at a time or all at once.

With a little imagination, you can use Find and Replace for other tasks as well. Here are some examples that should work in most word processors:

♦ Your friend created a long word processing document and used the word "pretty" (as in "pretty big," "pretty tired," and "pretty boring") in at least five dozen places. You want to remove this word. Use the Find and Replace feature to search for occurrences of the word "pretty" with a **Space** in front of it and replace it with nothing. Not only does this remove the word, but it ensures that spacing remains correct.

♦ Your friend also pressed **Return** twice at the end of each paragraph to add a blank line between paragraphs. You don't want the blank line. Use the Find and Replace feature to search for occurrences of two consecutive **Return** characters and replace them with one **Return** character.

♦ This same friend indented each paragraph by pressing the **Spacebar** five times. You'd rather use a **Tab** for this. Use the Find and Replace feature to search for occurrences of five consecutive **Spaces** and replace them with one **Tab**.

♦ This friend (to whom you really ought to give a copy of this book) also underlined all book and magazine names. You know that italics should be used for titles. Use the Find and Replace feature to search for occurrences of underlined characters and replace the bold style with italic style. (Be sure to turn off underlining at the same time.)

Use a Spelling Checker to Proofread

Typos are a common problem, even among the best typists. You can use the spelling check feature built into most word processors to check for typos.

One important thing to remember: A misspelled word that spells another word will not be caught by a spelling checker. For example, if you meant to type the word "if" and your fingers typed the word "of," the spelling checker will not notify you of the error. Always proofread your documents the old-fashioned way before distributing them.

Automation Tricks

. . . .

Ever stop to consider why you use a computer? There are many reasons, of course. Among them should be automation. When properly instructed, the computer can do things automatically for you. In this section, you'll see some examples of how you can automate tasks.

Use Publish and Subscribe

One of the great features of System 7 is called Publish and Subscribe. It enables you to create a document, "publish" it, and then have another document "subscribe" to it. This means that whatever information is in the published document—or *edition*, as it is called—automatically appears in the documents that subscribe to it. If the edition changes, the documents that subscribe to it also change as soon as the changes are saved. This works as long as the computer has access to the edition—even if that file is available on another computer connected via network!

Here's an example of Publish and Subscribe in which part of a small Microsoft Excel worksheet is incorporated into a Microsoft Word document. If you have these two programs, give this a try. Even if you don't have these two programs, you can probably follow along with one or two applications you do have.

1 In Microsoft Excel, create and save a small worksheet.

2 Use your mouse to select a portion of the worksheet to publish. It might look something like Figure 4.17.

3 Choose **Create Publisher** from the **Edit** menu.

4 Use the directory portion of the dialog box that appears to open a folder to save the edition into.

5 Enter a name for the edition.

6 Click **Publish**.

	A	B	C	D	E
1	Packing Peanut Sales				
2	Top 4 Salespeople				
3					
4	Division	Ralph	Tom	Mike	Total
5	East	514.00	145.00	487.00	1,146.00
6	West	256.00	359.00	358.00	973.00
7	North	1,245.00	845.00	647.00	2,737.00
8	South	124.00	488.00	1,778.00	2,390.00
9	Total	2,139.00	1,837.00	3,270.00	7,246.00
10					
11					
12					

Packing Peanuts Worksheet

Figure 4.17 Selecting a portion of an Excel worksheet to use as an edition file

7 If desired, choose **Quit** (**Command-Q**) from the **File** menu to quit Excel. If prompted to save changes, click **Yes**.

8 Create or open a Word document that you want to use the edition in.

9 Position the insertion point where you want the edition to appear.

10 Choose **Subscribe To** from the **Edit** menu.

11 Use the directory portion of the dialog box that appears to locate the Excel edition file you just created.

12 Select the file and click **Subscribe** to insert it in your document. It might look something like Figure 4.18.

13 Choose **Save** (**Command-S**) from the **File** menu to save the Word document with the edition incorporated into it.

To see how changes in the original worksheet file will affect the Word file that has subscribed to it, open the worksheet, make a change, and save it. When you look at the Word file, the new value automatically appears, as shown in Figure 4.18.

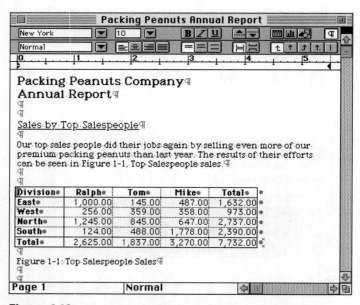

Figure 4.18 A Word document with an Excel edition incorporated into it

Create and Use Macros

A macro is a series of commands that can be automatically executed. They save you time by letting your Macintosh, which can work a lot faster than you, perform repetitive tasks. If a task is time consuming, you can instruct your Macintosh to complete it while you're away from the computer—perhaps even overnight. (Unlike most workers, your Macintosh will never demand overtime pay or coffee breaks.)

Macros or scripting capabilities are built into many applications, like Microsoft Word, Microsoft Excel, Claris FileMaker Pro, and Claris-Works. Whenever possible, take advantage of macro features to automate repetitive tasks. Here are some examples:

- ♦ Create a Microsoft Word script that automatically opens mail merge documents, merges the information, prints the completed letters, and deletes the data file. (Be careful with any macro that deletes files.)

- ♦ Create a Microsoft Excel macro that automatically imports mainframe information, parses it into columns, formats it, performs calculations on it, sorts it, and prints it in multipage formatted reports.

- ♦ Create a Claris FileMaker Pro script that automatically imports comma-delimited text files, eliminates unnecessary data, exports data into other FileMaker Pro files, and prepares reports from each file.

QuicKeys

If you want to get serious about automation, CE Software, Inc. has just the program for you: *QuicKeys*. This full-featured macro software package can automate virtually any repetitive task that you can perform on a Macintosh. Best of all, since it isn't application-specific, you can have it perform tasks with multiple applications, all within the same macro or "quickey." It even works with the voice recognition features built into some of the newer Macintosh models (like the AV machines) so you can put your Macintosh to work with a single word.

♦ Create a ClarisWorks macro that automatically converts curly quote characters in a document into standard quotes and then saves the file as a plain text document that can be read on any computer.

Miscellaneous Application Tricks

Here are a few other application tricks that really didn't fit into any of the other sections of this chapter. Just because they're last, don't think they're least useful.

Go Through the Tutorial

Need to learn a program fast? Go through the Tutorial or Getting Started section of its documentation. It's like attending self-paced, hands-on training class where you can learn what the program does and how it does it. Best of all, it comes free with many software packages.

Set Preferences to Customize

Most applications have a **Preferences** command that lets you customize the program for the way you like to work. Always take advantage of the options offered by this command. You could save yourself a lot of repetitive formatting and setup time when creating new documents.

Customize Menus and Toolbars

All applications have menus. Nowadays, many also have toolbars. But did you know that more than a few of these applications also give you a way to customize the menus and toolbars? Here are some examples in popular applications:

♦ Customize a Word menu by choosing **Commands** from the **Tools** menu. You can also add or remove Word menu commands by installing or removing Word plug-in modules.

♦ Customize an Excel toolbar by choosing **Toolbars** from the **Options** menu. You can also add or remove Excel menu commands by installing or removing add-in macros.

♦ Customize the Claris FileMaker Pro's **Scripts** menu by choosing **ScriptMaker** from the **Scripts** menu, creating a script, and setting it so it is displayed on the menu.

♦ Customize a ClarisWorks Shortcuts Palette by choosing **Edit Shortcuts** from the **Shortcuts** submenu under the **File** menu with the Shortcut Palette showing. (Use the **Shortcuts** submenu under the **File** menu to show the Shortcut Palette first, if necessary.)

Switch Applications

With more than one application open, there are three good ways you can switch from one to another:

♦ Use the System 7 **Application** menu to choose another open application. This is shown in Figure 4.19.

♦ Click anywhere in a window for another open application. If you want to make the Finder active, click anywhere on a Finder window or the Desktop.

♦ Hold down the **Option** key while clicking anywhere in a window for another open application. This not only switches to that application, but it hides the current application. If you want to make the Finder active and hide the current active application, hold down **Option** while clicking anywhere on a Finder window or the Desktop.

Figure 4.19 The System 7 Application menu lets you switch, hide, and show applications.

Hide Applications

If you have multiple applications open, your screen can soon become cluttered with windows.

♦ Use the **Hide** command under the System 7 **Application** menu (see Figure 4.19) to hide either the current application or all other applications.

♦ As discussed above, you can hide the current application while switching to another, by holding down the **Option** key while clicking in a window of the other application or while selecting its name from the System 7 **Application** menu.

♦ Use the **Show All** command under the System 7 **Application** menu to unhide all hidden applications.

Quit by Force

Here's the situation: You have three documents open in three different applications. Suddenly, while working with one application, your Macintosh freezes up. Your heart seems to stop because you haven't saved any of the open documents. What do you do?

The first thing you should try is the save command—press **Command-S** since you won't be able to use your mouse. Although this usually *doesn't* work, it is worth a try.

The next thing you can try is to Force Quit the application that froze. System 7 users can do this by pressing Command-Option-Esc. A Force Quit dialog box appears. Try clicking Cancel—you might get control of the program again. If that doesn't work, press Command-Option-Esc again and click Force Quit. If the problem is restricted to that program, the program should quit and you should regain control of your Macintosh. You should then save the other two documents and restart.

Some things to remember about the Force Quit command:

♦ Force-quitting doesn't always work. Sure, you'll usually get the Force Quit dialog box, but about half the time, neither the Force Quit nor Cancel button will work. That's when it's time to reach for the restart button or power switch.

◆ *Always* restart your Macintosh after force-quitting an application. When you use the Force Quit command, RAM gets messed up and weird things can start happening. Your Macintosh may not function reliably. By restarting, RAM is cleared out and you can start fresh.

◆ If you force-quit a program like FileMaker Pro which saves files automatically as it works, any open document files can be damaged. Of course, if you hit the power switch to restart without force-quitting, the same thing would happen. Just something to keep in mind.

Chapter 5

· · · · · · · · · · · · · · · · · · · ·

Telecommunications and Networking Tricks

Telecommunications is the process by which information can be transferred—either by voice or computer—over telephone lines. Sounds boring, doesn't it? In reality, telecommunications is one of the most interesting things you can do with your computer. It can open up the whole world to you.

This chapter will help you teach your Macintosh to communicate more effectively. You'll get some solid telecommunications tips and tricks for logging on, communicating effectively, and minimizing online time (to save money). You'll also learn tricks for using your fax modem, exchanging files between your Macintosh and non-Macintosh systems, and working with networks.

Telecommunications Basics

Telecommunications, as discussed in this chapter, refers mainly to using your computer to connect to another computer, known as the *remote* system. Once the two computers are connected, you can exchange information in the form of electronic mail messages, shareware and freeware files, and database contents.

This chapter is mostly concerned with two kinds of remote systems. One is a commercial online service like America Online, CompuServe, AppleLink, eWorld, or Prodigy. These services offer a wide variety of features but charge a fee for access. The fee can be based on actual usage, a monthly charge, or some combination of the two. The other kind of remote system is called a bulletin board system or BBS. BBSes are usually run by hobbyists and, due to limited size and resources, offer far fewer features than their commercial counterparts. There are well over 100,000 BBSes worldwide. Some of them charge a fee for access, some don't.

In order to connect to either kind of remote system, you need a computer, a modem, a phone line, and telecommunications software. You know what a computer and a phone line are. A *modem* is a device that turns the computer's outgoing digital signals into analog signals that can be transferred over phone lines and takes the remote computer's incoming analog transmissions and converts them back into digital signals that the computer can understand. Modems generally range in price from $50 to $500, depending on transfer speed capability (baud rate) and features. *Telecommunications software* controls the modem and acts as a translator between you and the signals going in and out of the modem. Some popular telecommunications software packages include David Alverson's *ZTerm* (shareware), Software Ventures Corporation's *MicroPhone*, Aladdin Systems' *SITComm*, and The Freesoft Company's *White Knight*.

Log On Tricks

You can't do much telecommunicating if you can't connect. Here are a few tips and tricks for finding and logging on to a remote system.

Find a BBS Near You

Finding a good, local BBS isn't always easy. Here are some tips:

♦ Start with a BBS list. You can often find these in books that discuss telecommunications. Write down numbers for at least ten systems. BBSes don't have long life spans and even the best BBS list is usually out of date within six months.

♦ Call BBSes. While online, look around for other BBS lists. BBSes are possibly the best sources of BBS lists. Download or capture any lists you find to review them offline.

♦ While online with a BBS, send a message to the appropriate public area asking if other callers know of any BBSes in the area. Most people don't call just one BBS. You might run into someone who knows of a system you can call near your home.

♦ When you log off or disconnect from a BBS, check the log off notes that appear on your screen. You'll often find area BBS phone numbers listed there.

♦ Although you can connect to almost any BBS with your Macintosh, you may want to concentrate on finding a good Macintosh BBS where you can find Macintosh-related message areas and shareware and freeware files. IBM BBSes tend to overlook the needs of Macintosh users.

Choose an Online Service That Meets Your Needs

Commercial online services offer far more than any BBS can offer. When choosing an online service to subscribe to, don't join one just because you saw an ad for it on television or your friend uses it. Find out what the service has to offer, how much it costs, and whether you can access it through a local network connection. Check into all the major services and compare. Then make your decision. Only computer book authors are crazy enough to subscribe to all the services.

Why a Local BBS?

A local BBS should be the first choice of anyone interested in telecommunications—especially beginners. Why? Here are a few reasons:

- Small local systems are generally easier to learn and use than massive commercial online services. They're a great place to get started with telecommunications.

- If a local system is within your local calling area, there are no phone charges for connecting with it.

- Local systems have information of interest to people in your area. You can meet other computer users—possibly people in your own town. The atmosphere is generally more friendly and intimate than on commercial online services.

- There is often no fee to access small local systems. This makes telecommunications very affordable. Even if there is a fee, it's usually much less than you'd have to pay for access to a commercial online service.

- Some local systems have quite a bit to offer, including access to worldwide networks like Fidonet, the Internet, and OneNet, to online games, and to tens of thousands of shareware and freeware files.

Buy the Fastest Modem You Can Afford

The speed of your modem will determine how quickly it (and you) can exchange information. Not long ago, the standard was 2400 baud or roughly 240 characters per second. Then it became 9600 baud (although some online services were slow to make the change). Many BBSes can support connections at 14400 baud, 19200 baud, and even faster.

Don't buy a modem for today's standard. Buy one for *tomorrow's* standard. A modem has virtually no moving parts and can last for years if taken care of properly. Saving a few dollars today can cost you a few dollars more tomorrow.

Buy a Fax Modem

If you're shopping for a modem, consider a fax modem. For not much more than the cost of a regular modem, you can buy one that can send and receive faxes. Some of them also include OCR (optical character recognition) software that'll enable your Macintosh to convert text in graphics to text you can manipulate with your word processor. Something to consider, isn't it?

Connect at a "Smart" Speed

Some commercial online services charge a different rate for high speed (over 2400 baud) connections. The rate may be roughly twice the rate for slower connections. Before you connect to one of these services, consider what you'll be doing while online.

♦ If you plan to connect to read and write messages online, search for information like stock prices, or do a little shopping, connect at the slower speed. These tasks require that you read and respond to on-screen prompts. Since the average person can't read much faster than 1200 to 2400 baud, accessing the system at 9600 baud for these tasks is pointless.

♦ If you plan to connect to download or upload files or capture and send messages prepared offline, connect at the higher speed. Exchanging prepared data requires much less interaction. You can send or receive data at four times the speed for only twice the price. That's a bargain.

Turn Off Call Waiting

If you have the phone company's call waiting service, be sure to disable it before you let your modem dial out to a remote system. Call waiting produces tones that your modem may "hear" as line noise or random characters. At high-speed transmissions, the modem could lose the connection.

While the codes to disable call waiting vary in different areas, *70 or 1170 usually does the trick. You can include this in the dialing string for your telecommunications software. In fact, some telecommunications software packages have an option just to disable call waiting. You can see an example of the option as presented in Aladdin Systems' SIT-Comm in Figure 5.1.

Turn Local Echo On or Off

Ever connect to a remote system and find that the characters you type don't appear on your screen? Or that each character you type appears twice on your screen?

This is a result of Local Echo being incorrectly set. Your telecommunications software should offer a way to set this properly. If the characters you type don't appear at all, turn Local Echo On. If the characters you type appear twice, turn Local Echo Off.

Saving Your Password

Many telecommunications software packages enable you to set up log on or connect scripts that include the remote system's name and phone number and your log on name and password. Think twice about including your password in one of these scripts! If you include your password in a script and someone else uses your Macintosh, they'll be able to use your account on the remote system. This could jeopardize the privacy of your electronic communication and enable someone to use a service on your dime.

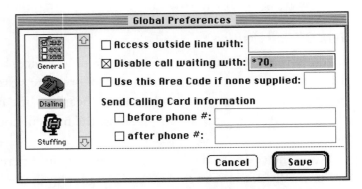

Figure 5.1 Include the codes to disable call waiting right in the dialing strings of software like Aladdin Systems' SITComm.

Communication Tricks

In this section, you'll find some tricks for getting the most out of an online service or BBS once you're connected.

Practice for Free

Although most commercial online services charge a fee based on access time, many services offer a free support or practice area. Once you've entered this area, you can spend as much time using the service as you want—without paying a dime. This is a great way to learn how to use a system without the clock ticking away. Here's how you can enter the free area on two popular online services:

♦ On America Online, choose **Members' Online Support** from the **Go To** menu. (Or use the Keyword **Help**.) When a dialog box appears asking you to confirm that you want to enter the free area, click **OK**.

♦ On CompuServe, enter **GO PRACTICE** at any system prompt and press **Return**.

Communicate with Others Worldwide — For the Cost of a Local Call

Most commercial online services and many BBSes reach computer users like you worldwide. They do this by offering their services throughout the world (like CompuServe does) or by connecting to worldwide networks like the Internet, Fidonet, or OneNet (just to name a few). On systems like these, when you write a message in a public forum, that message may be seen all over the world. In addition, if you have the user name or account number of a specific person on that system, you can exchange private messages with them. Contact friends or family members across the country, make business connections, and learn more about life in a foreign land—all for the cost of connecting to your local system.

Private Mail Isn't Always Private

The term "private mail" or "electronic mail" may lead you to believe that private mail messages sent electronically can only be read by the sender and recipient. This is not true. The administrator(s) of any online service or BBS may have the ability to read private mail messages. (This fact is usually posted on every system you dial into.) In addition, occasional system glitches can make the contents of private messages public. While administrators probably have better things to do with their time than read your mail and system glitches happen very infrequently, you should never include confidential information in a message. Ask yourself this question: "Would I want dozens (or even hundreds) of strangers to know this?" If the answer is no, don't send the information electronically.

E-Mail Anyone Through the Internet

You have an account on CompuServe. Your friend in Peoria has an account on America Online. Does this mean you can never exchange electronic mail? Of course not! Use the Internet gateway.

The Internet is a global network of computer systems, many of which are at colleges, universities, and research institutions. All major online services have "gateways" into the Internet. That means if you address a message correctly, it can travel through the Internet to the recipient. Depending on the kind of gateway and connection, messages can arrive less than an hour after they're sent—even if they have to travel across the country.

Table 5.1 lists many of the services you can exchange mail with through the Internet, the service's Internet address, and an example of an address to someone on that service. For more details on how you can use the Internet gateway from the service you subscribe to (America Online, CompuServe, GEnie, etc.), consult the online help area of that system, which is normally free of connect charges.

Table 5.1 Internet Addresses of Online Services and Networks

Service or Network	Internet Address	Example Address
America Online	aol.com	jdoe@aol.com
AppleLink	applelink.apple.com	jdoe@applelink.apple.com
AT&T Mail	attmail.com	jdoe@attmail.com (be sure to exclude any ! symbols that might be part of the address)
BITNET	append "bitnet" to the BITNET address	jdoe@pegasus.bitnet
BIX	bix.com	jdoe@bix.com
CompuServe	compuserve.com	12345.6789@compuserve.com (change the comma in the CompuServe address to a period)
CONNECT	connectinc.com	jdoe@connectinc.com
Delphi	delphi.com	jdoe@delphi.com
EasyLink	eln.attmail.com	62123456@eln.attmail.com
Fidonet	use the format "first_last@f<node>.n<net>.z<zone>.fidonet.org"	To send to John Doe, 1:123/456, address it: John_Doe@f456.n123.z1.fidonet.org
GEnie	genie.geis.com	jdoe@genie.geis.com
HandsNET	handsnet.org	HN1234@handsnet.org
MCI Mail	mcimail.com	0001234567@mcimail.com (be sure to pad any 7-digit user IDs to 10 digits with leading zeros)
Prodigy	prodigy.com	abcd12e@prodigy.com
The Well	well.sf.ca.us	jdoe@well.sf.ca.us

Use the Internet to Contact the White House and Congress

You can even send a message to the President or Vice President via the Internet. Here are their addresses:

president@whitehouse.gov
vice-president@whitehouse.gov

Many Congresspeople are also online. To learn more about how you can send messages through the Internet to members of the House of Representatives, send a message to:

comments@hr.house.gov

Use Smileys

"Joe doesn't know what he's talking about. He only wrote five books on the subject." Is the author of that comment being sarcastic? Or does he mean it? And what do you think Joe will say when he reads it?

One of the biggest problems with electronic communication is that the words you type into messages lack the visual and audible clues to meaning that are so important for communication. There are no facial expressions, no stressed words, no shouts. A comment you make as a joke might be taken very seriously since the reader can't see the wink you intended to go with it.

Smileys make it possible to accompany your written words with facial expressions. A smiley is a series of regular keyboard characters that represent facial expressions like smiles, winks, and frowns. There are hundreds of smileys; you can find lists of them on many online services and BBSes. Here is a list of the most basic ones—look at them sideways and you'll see the smile, wink, or frown. Use them in your messages to help readers understand what you're saying.

Smiley	Meaning
:-)	Smile
;-) or ,-)	Wink
:-p or ;-p	Sticking out tongue
:-(	Frown
:,(	Tears
:-o	Shout

Use Abbreviations

You can use a standard set of abbreviations to express yourself in electronic messages. While not as cute as smileys, some of these can express the same kinds of emotions. Others say much more with only a few characters. Here's a list of some of the most popular ones:

Abbreviation	Meaning
<g>	Grin
BTW	By the way
FWIW	For what it's worth
FYI	For your information
IMHO	In my humble opinion
LOL	Laughing out loud
ROFL	Rolling on the floor laughing
RTFM	Read the [censored by author] manual

One more thing to keep in mind: Typing your messages in all capital letters is considered shouting on online services and BBSes. Don't do it unless you really are shouting.

Pause, Continue, and Interrupt Text Streams

On a command line interface system, text may appear at the bottom of your telecommunications window and scroll up. Sometimes, it might scroll too fast to read it. Try these standard commands:

Keystroke	Command
Control-S	Pause text stream
Control-Q	Continue text stream
Control-C	Cancel text stream

Use a Graphic Interface

As a Macintosh user, you're accustomed to a graphic user interface. So why use a command line interface to communicate online? While most online services and BBSes are command line systems, there are plenty of systems that utilize a graphic user interface, complete with icons and menus. It's just a matter of looking for them.

- For a commercial online service, try America Online, e•World, AppleLink, and Prodigy. All of these systems have graphic user interfaces. The software you'll need to connect to these systems is usually provided free of charge or for a small setup fee, depending on the service.

- If you're a CompuServe user, check out a package called CompuServe Information Manager. This puts a graphic "front end" on CompuServe, making it somewhat easier to use. You can get this package from CompuServe.

- For BBSes, look for Macintosh-based systems on FirstClass, TeleFinder, or NovaLink Pro. The special software you'll need to take advantage of the graphic user interface is usually made available for free online; you can connect for the first time with any telecommunications software.

Online Time Tricks

While you're online with a commercial online service or BBS, the clock is ticking away. If the service you're connected to charges by the minute or if the telephone call you made to the service is outside your local calling area, each tick of the clock is money out of your pocket. Here are some tricks you can use to spend less time online—and save money.

Use Navigation Commands

A navigation command is any command you can type on an Online Service that takes you quickly to a specific area. The benefit of using these commands is that they let you avoid all the menus that would normally appear on the way to that area. If you make a list of the commands you need to visit the areas you use most, you can soon speed around any system, reducing online time.

- On America Online, use Keywords. Choose **Keyword** (**Command-K**) from the **Go To** menu. Type in a Keyword and click **OK**.

- On CompuServe, use Go commands. At any system prompt, type the word **GO** followed immediately by the name of the area you want to go to. Then press **Return**.

Customize the Go To Menu

You can take the above tip a step further for America Online. Version 2.0, or later, of its software lets you customize the **Go To** menu to include the places you visit most.

1 Choose **Edit Go To Menu** from the **Go To** menu.

2 In the **Goto Menu Editor** window that appears (see Figure 5.2), change or add menu entries and corresponding Keywords.

3 Click **Save Changes**.

The **Go To** menu immediately reflects the changes you made. In addition, you now have the ability to access up to ten favorite places with a keystroke.

Read and Write Messages Offline

One of the most time-consuming things you can do online is read and respond to messages. You can easily cut the amount of connect time by reading and writing messages offline. Here's how to do this on most systems.

1 Connect to the online service or BBS and navigate to the message area you want to read.

Key	Menu Entry	Keyword
⌘1	Computing & Software	Computing
⌘2	Online Clock	Time
⌘3	New Services	New
⌘4	Sign on a Friend	Friend
⌘5	File Search	Quickfinder
⌘6	Tech Live Auditorium	CS Live
⌘7		
⌘8		
⌘9		
⌘0		

Goto Menu Editor

Save Changes

Figure 5.2 Editing America Online's Go To menu

2 Turn on your telecommunications software's capture or save to text feature. (You can usually find this under the **File** menu, but it varies from program to program.) This feature enables you to save everything that scrolls by on your screen to a file on disk.

3 Instruct the online service or BBS to start displaying messages. If possible, display them continuously, without pauses. Don't worry about the information flying by faster than you can read it. It's all being saved to a file on disk.

4 If desired, navigate to other message areas you want to read and scroll those new messages by as well.

5 When you are finished "reading" messages, turn off the capture or save to text feature. (Again, the command to do this is usually under the **File** menu.)

6 Log off the system.

7 Use a text editor or word processor to open the capture file and read the messages. Take your time. There's no billing clock ticking now.

8 Write your responses to the messages you read. While you can write all the responses in one new file, you might find it easier to create a new file for each message you write. Save the file as a plain text file.

9 Log on to the service again. Navigate to the message area you want to send a message to. If you want to reply to a specific message, you can instruct the software to display that message.

10 Use the appropriate system command to tell the system you want to write a message or reply to the current message. Depending on the system, you may be asked if you want to send prepared message text. If so, say **yes** and use your telecommunications software to upload a text file containing the message text. If not, you can usually use copy and paste to paste the message text into the telecommunications window. Either way, you'll see the message entered right into the screen a lot faster than you could type it. When the message is finished, use the appropriate system command to send or save it. Do this for each message you want to send, then log off.

One important thing to keep in mind here: some BBS software packages are picky about having blank lines in a message. Blank lines sometimes signal the end of a message. If you want to use blank lines between paragraphs in your messages, type a space onto the line. It'll look blank, but the BBS won't see it as blank.

Experiment with this until you get the hang of it. It can save a lot of time if done right.

Compress Files

Sending files to a remote system? Compress them first! Compression software packages like Aladdin Systems' *StuffIt Deluxe*, Bill Goodman's

---

FlashMail and CompuServe Navigator

America Online, CompuServe, and other online services offer easy ways to read and write messages offline. Here are two examples:

- *FlashMail* is a feature of America Online. It makes it possible to have your Macintosh dial in automatically, retrieve messages, and send messages you wrote offline. A typical FlashMail session can take only a few minutes to exchange dozens of messages. Flash-Mail is part of the America Online software which comes free to subscribers. One drawback: It doesn't enable you to exchange messages with forums—only individual accounts.

- *The CompuServe Navigator* is a software package available from CompuServe. Set it up to log on, collect messages and send messages in any forum, search libraries, download and upload files, and perform other tasks—all automatically. When it's finished with a session, view the results in a **Review** window. The main benefit of the Navigator is that it completely removes you from the hassle of dealing with CompuServe's somewhat complex command line interface. You can speed through the system without knowing a single command, snatching up messages and files on the way. Any serious CompuServe user should consider this package.

Compact Pro, and Now Software's *Now Compress*, can reduce the size of an average file by 50 to 80 percent. Smaller files take less time to transfer, saving you time and money.

Self-Extracting Archives

Most compression software packages offer the ability to create self-extracting archive (or SEA) files. This makes it possible for the file's recipient to open (or decompress) the file without special software. The trouble with SEAs is that the self-extraction code can add from 12 to 20 K to the file's size. When compressing a small (say, 25 K) file, you can actually end up with a compressed SEA that's bigger than the original file!

Don't create SEAs unless you know that the file's recipient doesn't have the appropriate compression or decompression software. The "expand only" versions of compression software are freely distributable. If you know you'll be sending a lot of files to one recipient, why not send him a SEA containing the "expand only" version of the compression software? From then on, you can send him regular compressed files and save 12 to 20 K per file transfer.

One more thing: Most BBSes do not allow uploads in SEA format. The reason: If a BBS system operator has 1,000 files, each 15 K larger than they need to be, he or she needs 15 MB more disk space to store them. That's a lot to ask of someone who might be on a tight budget!

Use the Best File Transfer Protocol

When transferring files, you'll find that certain file transfer protocols are more efficient than others. ZModem is among the quickest and it has the added ability to continue file transfers that have been interrupted. XModem with 1 K blocks is a good second choice. Just remember that whichever file transfer protocol you choose, the selection must be the same on both the sending and receiving ends.

Turn Off Instant Messages

Instant Messages is a feature of America Online that makes it possible to send and receive brief messages immediately to anyone online. When you send an Instant Message, a message window appears on the recipient's screen. Of course, when you receive an Instant Message, that window appears on *your* screen, interrupting whatever you were doing. If you're in a hurry to get something done on America Online, receiving a flood of Instant Messages can be downright annoying.

You can turn Instant Messages on or off by sending an Instant Message. Here's how:

1. To turn off or "ignore" Instant Messages, choose **Send Instant Message** (**Command-I**) from America Online's **Members** menu.

2. In the **Name** edit box, enter the following, exactly as it appears here: $im_off

3. In the body of the message, type anything. It doesn't matter—whatever you type won't really be sent. (See Figure 5.3 for a creative example.) If you leave the body of the message blank, you may get a dialog box telling you that you can't send an empty Instant Message.

4. Click **Send**. A dialog box appears with the following message: "You are now ignoring Instant Messages." Click **OK** to dismiss it and continue working.

5. To stop ignoring Instant Messages, choose **Send Instant Message** (**Command-I**) from the **Members** menu.

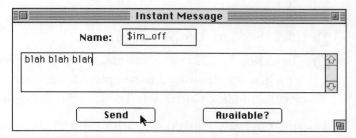

Figure 5.3 Sending an Instant Message to turn off Instant Messages

6 In the **Name** edit box, enter the following, exactly as it appears here: $im_on

7 In the body of the message, type anything; remember, you can't leave it blank.

8 Click **Send**. A dialog box appears with the following message: "You are no longer ignoring Instant Messages." Click **OK** to dismiss it and continue working.

Use the Download Manager

The Download Manager is a feature of America Online that makes downloading files a bit more convenient. Use it to download batches of files together. This way, you can pick out a bunch of files to download, tell your America Online software to download it, and leave your Macintosh unattended while it works. It'll even log off for you when it's done. Here's how:

1 View the description for a file you want to download.

2 Click the **Download Later** button.

3 A dialog box with the following message appears: "This file has been added to your list of files for later downloading." Click the **OK** button to continue choosing files to download.

4 Repeat steps 1 through 3 for each file you want to download.

5 To begin the download, choose **Download Manager** from the **File** menu.

6 The dialog box that appears, which is illustrated in Figure 5.4, shows all the files you've selected to download. You can use buttons to view file descriptions, delete files from the list, and perform other tasks.

7 Click the **Start Download** button.

8 The dialog box that appears has a check box you can use to log off when the download is completed. Turn that check box on or off and click **Continue**. The download begins.

America Online's FlashMail feature also enables you to download files. If this option is turned on, whatever files are listed in the Download Manager will be downloaded as part of your FlashMail session.

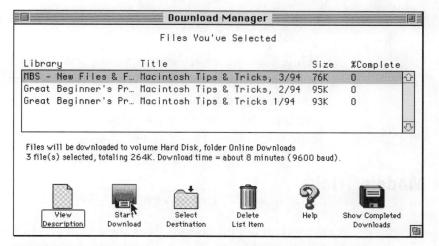

Figure 5.4 America Online's Download Manager window

Do Several Things at Once

Some online services and BBSes enable you to perform more than one task at a time. FirstClass is an example. When you connect to a FirstClass system with the FirstClass Client software, you can upload and download files, read and write messages, and even participate in a chat—all at the same time. Take advantage of this capability to read and write messages while exchanging files to save time online.

Stay Online for Free

If you want to stay connected to a commercial online service but don't plan to actively use it for a while, try entering the service's free area (mentioned earlier in this chapter). The billing clock stops but you remain connected so you don't have to log back on later on. When you're ready to actively use the service again, simply exit the free area and get back to work.

Some things to keep in mind if you do this:

♦ On most services, the free area isolates you from the rest of the system, so you won't be notified about incoming mail or other callers trying to contact you.

♦ Your phone will be tied up the entire time you're connected so you won't be able to use it to make or receive other calls.

♦ Some systems may automatically log you off after a certain period of inactivity.

♦ While you're connected, there's one less network connection available for other callers. If everyone did this all the time, it would soon be very difficult for callers to connect. Don't be selfish—use this trick only when you need to and for short periods of time.

Fax Modem Tricks

A fax modem is a modem that has the added ability to send and receive fax transmissions. Fax modem software usually works like a printer driver: You select it from the **Chooser** and then "print" to the fax modem. This makes it very easy to send documents you have prepared on your Macintosh. (Of course, it also makes it nearly impossible to send documents you haven't prepared on your Macintosh.) In this section, you'll find some tips for using your fax modem.

Send Faxes at Night

Telephone rates are cheapest at night. This is a fact of life. If you need to send a fax to someone outside your local calling area, try to send it after 11:00 P.M. Of course, you'll have to leave your computer and fax modem on to do this, but there's a trick for having it shut down automatically, too.

1 Set up the fax(es) to be sent at night.

2 At the end of the day, choose **Shut Down** from the Finder's **Special** menu. Depending on your fax modem and software, you may get a message like the one in Figure 5.5 giving you the opportunity to instruct your Macintosh to shut down after the fax(es) have been sent.

3 Click **Shut Down When Finished**. Your Macintosh will attempt to send the fax(es) and shut down afterwards.

> ⚠ There are 1 items in your fax queue.
> If you Shut Down now, these items will be sent
> when you restart the computer. Do you want
> TelePort to Shut Down after the 1 items have been
> sent ?
>
> [**Shut Down Now**]   [**Shut Down When Finished**]

Figure 5.5 Your software may offer to shut down your Macintosh after sending faxes at night.

Use Small Cover Sheets—Or None at All

Fancy cover sheets are very popular with people who want to prove that they're imaginative individuals. If your faxes can speak for themselves, use the smallest fax cover sheet you can—or none at all. Why? Because every inch of fax you send takes time to send and uses paper on the recipient's fax machine. Why waste time and paper?

Choose Your Fax Modem Driver with a Keystroke

Some fax modem software—like the software that comes with Global Village Communications' Teleport fax modems—include hot keys to choose the fax modem driver. Check the documentation that came with your fax modem software to see if it also uses this feature. If not, use a program like CE Software's *QuicKeys* or Now Software's *NowMenus* to assign a keystroke to switch to the fax modem driver. This saves time over using the **Chooser**.

Set Up a Fax Schedule for Incoming Faxes

If your fax modem is your only fax machine and it does not have a dedicated phone line, be sure to tell the people who send you faxes that they either have to call you before sending a fax or fax during a certain time each day. For example, if you work a standard 9 to 5 day (lucky you), you might want to leave your Macintosh on overnight and accept faxes from 5:00 P.M. to 9:00 A.M. This way you won't answer the phone and get a fax tone screaming in your ear.

Use a Fax Modem and OCR to Retype Text

You've got a copy of your company's annual report. You want to include the text and financial reports in another document. Do you start retyping? If you've got a fax modem and OCR software, the answer is no!

1 If necessary, photocopy the original document so that it's on flat paper. (You can't squeeze a booklet into a fax machine feeder, can you?)

2 Fax the pages of the document from a standard fax machine to your fax modem. It's vital that you feed the pages in as straight as possible! In addition, if the sending fax machine has a "fine" or "best" setting, make sure that it's selected.

3 Open the incoming fax document on your Macintosh and put the OCR software to work translating the graphic text to editable text.

This isn't a foolproof method of converting printed documents to editable text, but it is effective. You'll have to proofread the results carefully—a spelling checker in your word processing software can help identify spelling mistakes that occur when the OCR software makes an error. If you only have a page or two of text to convert, do yourself a favor and just type it in. You might spend more time messing around with the OCR software than you would take to just type it in the first place.

Use a Scanner

If your fax modem is your only fax machine, you might find it tough to fax documents that you haven't created on your Macintosh. This is possibly the biggest drawback to fax modems. If you have a scanner, however, you can use it to scan documents into your Macintosh. Once on disk, you can then fax the document anywhere you like.

Cross-Platform Communications Tricks

You've got a Macintosh at work. John, who works down the hall, has an IBM running Windows. And your home computer is an old Apple IIgs. How can you get files you create at home onto John's computer?

This section will tell you how by providing a few tricks to transfer files from one computer platform to another.

Use a Modem to Exchange Files

One of the best things about telecommunications is that modems and phone lines don't care what kind of computers are connected to them. This makes it possible for a Macintosh to dial into a non-Macintosh computer and exchange files with it.

1 Connect both computers to modems and phone lines and turn them on.

2 On one computer, start the telecommunications software and instruct it to answer the phone.

3 On the other computer, start the telecommunications software and instruct it to dial the other computer. The two computers should connect.

Filenames

Macintosh users are spoiled: We can name our files with up to 31 characters. Folks in the DOS world are limited to eight characters followed by a period (or "dot") and a three-character "extension." The extension can sometimes be very important for DOS users. Since their files don't have type and creator codes built into them like Macintosh files do, some of their software products rely on the extension to tell them what kind of file a file is.

When naming files that will ultimately be read on IBM-compatible computers, stick to DOS filename conventions. Otherwise filenames may be truncated and extensions may be missing. Here are a few DOS filename rules:

- A filename may be from one to eight characters long, optionally followed by a period and then a one to three character extension.
- Filenames may not contain spaces or symbol/punctuation characters other than these: ! @ # $ % & ( ) - _ { } '
- The following extensions should not be used for plain document files: COM, EXE, BAS, SYS, and BAT.

④ Instruct one computer to send the file you need on the other computer.

⑤ Instruct the other computer to receive the file being sent. (If you're using ZModem, you might not even need to do this step; the software may sense the file coming and accept it automatically.)

⑥ Repeat steps 4 and 5 for each file you need to transfer.

⑦ When you are finished, use the appropriate commands to disconnect (or hang up) on each computer.

Use a Null Modem Cable to Exchange Files

A null modem cable is a serial cable you can use to connect the serial ports of two computers. The cable needs to have the correct pin configuration on both ends so you can plug it into two different systems. Once connected, use telecommunication software on both computers to send and receive files. It works much like sending files via modem, but there isn't any modem.

Read and Write to DOS Disks

If you've got a Macintosh with a SuperDrive (basically any Macintosh made after March, 1989), you can read and write to DOS-compatible disks. Apple even provides the software to do this: Apple File Exchange.

① Launch Apple File Exchange. Its main window, illustrated in Figure 5.6, appears. The contents of your hard disk are displayed in the directory window on the left.

② Insert a DOS-formatted disk. Your Macintosh reads the disk and displays its contents in the directory window on the right. This is also illustrated in Figure 5.5. As you can see, DOS subdirectories appear as folders.

③ The **Mac to MS-DOS** and **MS-DOS to Mac** menus let you choose from among the translators that you have in the Apple File Exchange folder. These translators sometimes come with software applications, but since many applications have translators built in, Apple File Exchange translators are getting tougher and tougher to find. For plain text files or files that

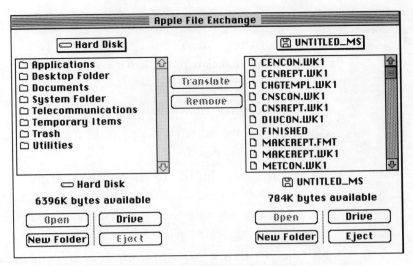

Figure 5.6 Apple File Exchange's main window

have identical formats on either platform (like many Microsoft products), special translators aren't necessary at all; you can use the **Default Translation**.

4 To copy a file from your Macintosh to the DOS disk, use the left side directory window to find the file. Click on it once to select it. To select multiple files, hold down the **Command** key while clicking on each one. Then click the **Translate** button.

5 To copy a file from the DOS disk to your Macintosh, use the right side directory window to find the file. Click on it once to select it. To select multiple files, hold down the **Command** key while clicking on each once. Then click the **Translate** button.

6 You can use the **Eject** button to eject the DOS disk and insert another if you need to. You can also use the **New Folder** button to create a new folder on either the Macintosh disk or the DOS disk. On the DOS disk, this will become a *subdirectory*.

7 When you are finished, click **Quit**. If a DOS disk is still in the disk drive, it is ejected.

Format DOS Disks

You can also format disks in a DOS-readable format using Apple File Exchange. This makes it possible for you to create disks for other computer systems.

1 Launch Apple File exchange.

2 Insert an unformatted floppy disk. A dialog box like the one in Figure 5.7 appears.

3 Use the radio button to choose the appropriate capacity for the disk. Options in the scrolling list of formats turn black or gray depending on what you select. Click the one for **MS-DOS** when it is black to select it.

4 Click **Initialize**. Your Macintosh begins the initialization process. When it is finished, the new blank disk appears in the right side directory window of Apple File Exchange.

Decompress DOS-Compressed Files

Like Macintosh files, DOS files can be compressed. The trouble is, compression schemes popular on DOS-based systems—like ZIP and ARC—aren't the same as ones on Macintosh systems. And since your Macintosh can't run an IBM-based program without a little help (like emulation software or hardware), you might one day find yourself with a file you can't read.

Fortunately, Macintosh shareware programmers have come up with Macintosh-compatible software products that can decompress these

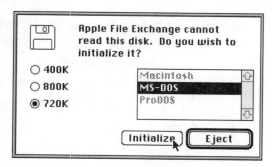

Figure 5.7 Initializing a disk with Apple File Exchange

Apple File Exchange, PC Exchange, MacLink Plus, AccessPC, and DOS Mounter

Apple File Exchange is the software Apple provides for free to exchange files between Macintosh computers and MS-DOS or ProDOS (Apple //) disks. It has few bells and whistles and isn't very glamorous, but it has two big things going for it: It works and it's free.

If you regularly exchange files between your Macintosh and IBM-compatible computers, you may want to look into a few products that let you insert, read, write to, and format DOS disks without launching any special applications. Some examples are Apple Computer's *PC Exchange*, DataViz Inc.'s *MacLink Plus*, Insignia Solutions' *AccessPC*, and Dayna Communications, Inc.'s *DOS Mounter*. These programs use control panels to be able to read and translate DOS disk files on the fly. You might find this a lot quicker and easier than reaching for Apple File Exchange.

files. *ZipIt* by Tommy Brown is one. Not only does it let you decompress files compressed with the ZIP compression scheme, but it lets you create ZIP-compressed files as well. You can find this program and others like it on online services and BBSes.

Networking Tricks

In this section, you'll find a few tricks to make networking Macintoshes a bit easier.

Use an Alias to Mount a Network Volume

For a quick and easy way to mount a network volume, make an alias of that volume and store it on your Desktop or under your **Apple** menu. Then, when you open the alias, it automatically mounts the volume. Of course, if there's password protection on the volume, you'll still have to enter the appropriate user name and password before you can use it.

Use an Alias to Open a Folder on a Network Volume

Taking the previous trick a step further, if you need to open a specific folder buried inside a network volume, you can create an alias for that folder. When you open the alias, it not only mounts the volume, but it opens the folder. Remember, you may still have to type in your user name and password if the volume is password protected.

Use File Sharing to Network

System 7 File Sharing is possibly the simplest and least expensive form of networking available. While it isn't necessarily fast, it may be enough to meet the networking needs of many small businesses. Here are a few tips for File Sharing networks:

♦ To force a registered user to log on as a Guest, open the **Users & Groups** control panel, double-click the user's account icon to open it, and turn off the check box for **Allow user to connect**. This makes it possible to restrict access temporarily without deleting the user's account.

♦ To prevent nonregistered users from connecting, open the Users & Groups control panel, double-click the **Guest** account icon to open it, and turn off the check box for **Allow guests to connect**.

♦ To disconnect a user who is currently sharing a file, open the **File Sharing Monitor** control panel, click on the name of the user you want to disconnect, and click **Disconnect**. Keep in mind that this won't stop the user from reconnecting. To prevent the user from connecting again, you must change his privileges in the **Users & Groups** control panel.

♦ To automatically mount shared folders or volumes at startup, turn on the check box beside the item name in the **Chooser** dialog box that displays items you can connect to. If you do not have the **Save My Name and Password** option selected, you'll have to provide a password when connecting.

AppleTalk Remote Access

Apple's AppleTalk Remote Access (ARA) is a program you can use to create a mini-network between one Macintosh and another. When your Macintosh dials into another via ARA, a modem, and a phone line, the icon for the remote Macintosh's hard disk appears on your Desktop. You can open it and work on any file.

For best results, ARA requires that both computers have modems with speeds of at least 9600 baud. System 7, File Sharing, and ARA must be installed on both machines. And, of course, the remote Macintosh's modem must be set to answer the phone.

ARA is intended for PowerBook users who need to access their desktop Macintosh while traveling. Even if you don't have a PowerBook, you can probably come up with a few ideas for using ARA to connect Macintoshes and exchange files.

Chapter 6

. . . .

Hardware Tricks

Chapter 4 began by saying that a computer is completely useless without software. Well, the opposite is also true: Software is completely useless without computer hardware. In this chapter, you'll find some tips and tricks for keeping your hardware in good working order. You'll also find tricks for upgrading your system.

RAM Tricks

. . . .

Chapter 3 offered some RAM-related software tricks. In this section, you'll find some hardware tricks for installing RAM and disposing of old chips.

 ### Buy the Right SIMMs

Macintosh RAM comes on special chips called SIMMs: Single Inline Memory Modules. SIMMs have various capacities ranging from 256 K to 16 MB. Nowadays, 1 MB, 2 MB, and 4 MB SIMMs are most commonly used. SIMMs also have various speeds, measured in nanoseconds

(NS), the lowest being the fastest. The higher the capacity and the faster the speed, the more expensive the SIMM.

Common sense may tell you to buy the slowest, lowest capacity SIMMs you need to upgrade your Macintosh. While this can save you money now, it might cost you money in the future if you decide to sell your current machine and buy a new (or pre-owned) one. For example, say you have a Macintosh IIcx with 4 MB of RAM and you want to upgrade to 8 MB. A IIcx can use 100 NS SIMMs, but not many newer models can. That means you won't be able to take the 100 NS SIMMs out of your IIcx and install them in a newer machine. You'll have to buy new SIMMs again. You might avoid this problem by buying the fastest SIMMs you can afford. In many cases, there isn't even much of a price difference.

Install it Yourself

RAM isn't difficult to install, especially in the newer, modular Macintosh models. Some organizations that sell SIMMs provide free illustrated guides, videos, or tools to make it even easier for beginners. By installing SIMMs yourself, you can save $50 or more—the cost of having an authorized Apple dealer or a private consultant do it for you.

If you do decide to install your own SIMMs, keep these important points in mind:

- Turn off your Macintosh and disconnect the power before opening your computer.

- Do not use magnetized tools to work on your Macintosh.

- Discharge static electricity and ground yourself before opening your Macintosh or touching any chips or internal parts.

- In early Macintosh II, IIx, IIcx, IIci, and IIfx models, Apple used plastic tabs on the SIMM slots. If your Macintosh has these tabs, be careful when removing or inserting SIMMs. The plastic tabs are very easy to break and can be costly to replace.

Add RAM Slots

If your Macintosh has eight SIMM slots (two banks of four), and you want more than 8 MB of RAM, you'd normally need to buy four 2 MB or larger SIMMs and use them to replace four 1 MB SIMMs already in your Macintosh. The SIMMs you'd remove would be useless.

MicroMac Technologies makes SIMMdoubler II, a device that enables you to put two SIMMs in the same slot. With it—or a similar product—you can increase the amount of RAM in your Macintosh with less expensive SIMMs (1 MB SIMMs are considerably cheaper than 2 MB or 4 MB SIMMs) and without discarding any SIMMs.

Give Your Old SIMMs a New Home

What do you do with old 256 K and 512 K SIMMs that are just about useless these days? Here are two suggestions:

- ♦ Donate them to a school or other nonprofit organization. Not only will you be extending the life of these chips, but you might even be able to deduct a portion of their value on your income tax return. (Ask your accountant.)
- ♦ Make jewelry out of them. Imagine how different a pair of SIMM earrings or a SIMM tie clasp would look at the next party you attend!

Hard Disk Tricks

Chapter 2 offered some software-related tips for dealing with disks. Here are some hardware tips and tricks you can use to get more out of your hard disk—or to add additional ones.

Partition Large Hard Disks

Because minimum file size depends on the size of a disk's partitions, partition hard disks that will be used to store small files. For example, say you have a 600 MB hard disk that will be used as a file server for your company's electronic mail system. Electronic mail messages are normally small files, 2 or 3 K in size. Yet if you do not partition the hard disk, each file will occupy a minimum of 9.5 K of hard disk space. The difference between the actual file size and the amount of space it takes up because of allocation block size is wasted. With

What's All This About Partitions and Allocation Blocks?

Partitioning is part of the hard disk initialization or logical formatting process. A partition is a usable area of disk with its own directory entries. A hard disk can have one or more partitions. A hard disk with multiple partitions will appear as multiple icons on your desktop even though they share one SCSI ID.

The size of a hard disk partition determines the size of its allocation blocks. An allocation block is the smallest amount of disk storage space your Macintosh can recognize. It's based on sectors, which are equal to 512 bytes. An allocation block can be one, two, or more sectors in size. An allocation block is also the smallest amount of disk storage space a file can occupy—a file can never be smaller than the size of the allocation blocks of the disk it's stored on. Therefore, if an allocation block is two sectors, the minimum file size is 1024 bytes or 1 K, even if the file is a simple text file with only one character in it.

The larger the hard disk partition, the larger the allocation block size. The following table provides some standard disk sizes and the size of allocation blocks in each. To calculate the allocation block size in kilobytes for a hard disk not included in this table, take the total disk capacity in kilobytes, divide it by 32,767, round the result up to the nearest whole number, and then multiply it by .5. (Never said it would be easy.)

Hard Disk Size	Allocation Block Size
20 MB	.5 K
40 MB	1 K
80 MB	1.5 K
100 MB	2 K
120 MB	2 K
170 MB	3 K
230 MB	3.5K

Hard Disk Size	Allocation Block Size
340 MB	5.5 K
600 MB	9.5 K
1 GB	16 K

This also explains why a tiny file on a 600 MB hard disk can occupy 9.5 K of disk space on that disk and only 1 K of disk space when copied onto a floppy disk.

You can partition a hard disk with the formatting software that came with the disk. *Apple HD SC Setup*, which is part of the System Software, can format and partition disks that come with Apple computers. For non-Apple disks, try FWB Incorporated's *Hard Disk Toolkit* or LaCie Inc.'s *Silverlining*.

5,000 messages, that can easily add up to 30 or 40 MB of unusable space. If you partition the hard disk into two or three separate volumes, however, you reduce the minimum file size. This is a much more effective use of hard disk space.

Find and Use Hidden Hard Disk Space

If your hard disk was formatted with Apple HD SC Setup, there's a chance that you're missing out on some of the disk's storage capacity. This is because of the way Apple HD SC Setup initializes a disk. You can look for this hidden space by following these steps:

1. Start your Macintosh with the Disk Tools disk that came with your System software.

2. Launch **Apple HD SC Setup**.

3. Click the **Partition** button.

4. Click the **Custom** button. A map of the disk's partitions, like the one in Figure 6.1, appears. It shows the Mac Driver and hard disk partitions created by Apple HD SC Setup. It may also show a gray area at the bottom of the map. This gray area is unused space. On the 40 MB Connor drive that came with a

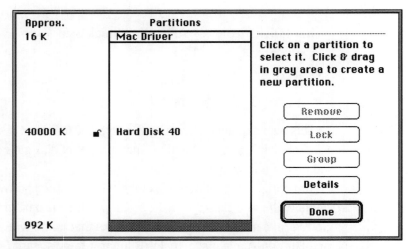

Figure 6.1 **Finding hidden hard disk space with Apple HD SC Setup**

Macintosh LC, this space amounted to a whopping 992 K—almost a full megabyte!

5 Click **OK** to close the partition map window.

6 Click **Done**.

7 Click **Quit**.

To use this space, you'll have to repartition the hard disk. *Back up the entire hard disk first.* Then follow these steps:

1 Start your Macintosh with the Disk Tools disk that came with your System software.

2 Launch **Apple HD SC** Setup.

3 Click the **Partition** button.

4 Click the **Custom** button.

5 Click on the name of the hard disk in the hard disk partition area to select it.

6 Click **Remove** to remove the partition. You'll see a warning message telling you that the data in the partition will be destroyed. Click **OK** *only* if you have backed up the disk as instructed above!

7 With your mouse, drag in the gray area from a position just below the Mac Driver partition on the map down to the bottom of the map. You'll see the size of the new partition indicated on the left side of the map window.

8 When you let go of the mouse button, a new window appears so you can select the type of partition. Select **Macintosh Volume**.

9 Make sure the value in the size edit box is equal to all available disk space. If it isn't, you can type in a new value.

10 Click **OK**.

11 When the message "Partitioning was Successful" appears, click **Done**.

12 Click **Quit**.

If you use formatting software like those products mentioned earlier in this chapter, you won't have to go through all this trouble. It's only Apple HD SC Setup that sometimes hides disk space.

Use Compression Software to Increase Disk Space

The best way to increase available disk space in a hard disk is to delete the files you don't need. But what if that isn't enough? That's when you might want to look into compression software.

There are two kinds of compression software that can help you get more data on a hard disk:

♦ File compression software can compress files in the background while your Macintosh is idle, then decompress them automatically when you need them. Examples of some popular packages include Aladdin Systems' *StuffIt SpaceSaver*, Now Software Inc.'s *Now Compress*, and Fifth Generation Systems' *AutoDoubler*.

♦ Disk compression software changes the hard disk drivers to fool them into thinking that the hard disk is larger than it really is. The result: The available hard disk space increases. Examples of some popular packages include Golden Triangle's *TimesTwo* and Alysis Software Corp.'s *eDisk*.

Upgrade Your Hard Disk

When all else fails and you need more disk space than you can squeeze out of your hard disk, it's time to upgrade. You have two main options when you buy a new hard disk: internal or external. Here are the pros and cons of each if you have to decide:

♦ Internal hard disks are generally $50 to $150 cheaper than external hard disks. Why? Because there's no need to provide you with a case, power supply, and internal cables. The drawback to buying an internal hard disk is that you must use it inside your Macintosh (or inside an external hard disk case you already have). This means that whatever hard disk is inside your Macintosh has to come out. If there's no case to put it in, it can't be used.

♦ External hard disks may cost more money, but they make it possible to have and use multiple hard disks. Simply use a SCSI cable to plug the new external hard disk into your Macintosh. If properly formatted and turned on before startup, it appears as a new volume on your Desktop. If you want to get fancy, swap disks. For example, if you have an internal 40 MB hard disk and just purchased an external 170 MB hard disk, there's nothing to stop you from putting the 170 inside your Macintosh and the 40 inside the case the 170 came in. The result of this juggling: You have the larger disk inside your Macintosh and can keep the external around as a "spare."

Give Your Old Hard Disk a New Life

Want to know what to do with a hard disk you pull out of your Macintosh? Here are two suggestions:

♦ Buy an external hard disk case. Prices range from $75 to $150. Install the old internal hard disk into the case and use it as an external hard disk. It's great for backing up documents!

♦ Donate it to a school or other nonprofit organization. They'll be grateful for your generosity and you might be able to write off the contribution on your tax return. (Ask your accountant.)

SCSI Rules and Regulations SCSI or Small Computer Systems Interface is the standard connection for external hard disks; CD-ROM, SyQuest, and Bernoulli drives; and some printers and scanners. It's a great system on the Macintosh because you can "daisy-chain" up to six of these devices on your Macintosh's one SCSI port.

SCSI does have some rules, however. Here they are:

- Each device on the SCSI chain must have a different SCSI ID number. Your Macintosh CPU is always number 7. Your internal hard disk is normally number 0. That leaves numbers 1 through 6 for external SCSI devices. You can usually set the SCSI ID on an external device with a setting switch. If a switch isn't provided or not connected properly, you can set the SCSI ID with jumpers on the device itself.

- A SCSI chain must be terminated at both ends. Your computer has internal termination at one end and, if you don't have any devices connected to its SCSI port, it's internally terminated after the internal hard disk. Otherwise, the last device in the chain must have an internal or external terminator.

- The total length of cable on a SCSI chain should not exceed 18 feet. This is what Apple recommends, but, in reality, you might find the length a lot shorter. As a result, you should always use the shortest SCSI cable you can to connect devices.

- Interference from fluorescent lighting can cause SCSI problems (as well as problems with networking cables and the like), especially if low-quality cables are used. Try to use double-shielded cables whenever possible. They cost more, but they can save a lot of headaches.

Floppy Disk Tricks

• •

Chapter 2 also offered some software-related floppy disk tips and tricks. Here are some for floppy disk hardware.

Lock Disks

Although locking disks was mentioned in Chapter 2, it's worthwhile mentioning it here again. When you lock a floppy disk, you use hardware to prevent the disk from being written to by the computer. It is *impossible* for a fully functioning floppy disk drive to write to a locked floppy. That's one surefire way to protect floppies against computer viruses.

Use High-Density Disks in Low-Density Drives

Ever find yourself in a situation where you've got an old Macintosh with a low-density disk drive (like a Plus or SE) but the only disk you've got handy is a high-density disk? Here are some tips for dealing with this situation.

- If the disk is blank, you can format it in the low-density drive as a single-sided or double-sided disk. You can then copy files to it just as if it were a low-density disk.

- Once you've formatted a high-density disk as a low-density disk, you must "fool" a Macintosh SuperDrive into recognizing the disk as a low-density disk before it can read it. Otherwise, you'll get a message like the one in Figure 6.2. To fool it, put some adhesive tape over the hole opposite the disk lock tab on the disk. Then, when you stick the disk into the SuperDrive, your Macintosh will think it's a low-density disk.

- If the disk was already formatted as a high-density disk and has information on it that you need in the older Macintosh, you might be sunk. Find a Macintosh with a SuperDrive, copy the

Figure 6.2 The message displayed when you insert a high-density disk formatted as a low-density disk in a SuperDrive

Why Adhesive Tape Can Fool Your Macintosh

In case you're wondering why the above adhesive tape trick works, here's the explanation. SuperDrives use a sensor to determine whether a disk is a high-density or low-density disk. The sensor is a mechanical pin that pokes up—you guessed it—through the hole opposite the disk lock tab. If the hole is covered, the disk "feels" the same as a low-density disk as far as your Macintosh is concerned. That's how it's fooled.

information onto its hard disk. Then put some adhesive tape over the hole opposite the disk lock tab on the disk, insert the disk, and initialize it as a single- or double-sided disk. You can then copy the files back to the disk and use them in the old Macintosh.

Some folks say this isn't foolproof or reliable, so don't make a habit of doing it. In a pinch, it certainly can be helpful.

Monitor Tricks

Your Macintosh "talks" to you through its monitor by displaying what it's doing in windows and asking questions in dialog boxes (why do you think they call them that, anyway?). Keeping your monitor in good shape is important if you want to keep communicating with your Macintosh. Here are a few tips and tricks for doing just that.

Use a Practical Screen Saver

Screen savers can be very entertaining these days, offering popular cartoon characters, voyages to the final frontier, flying appliances, and bubbling aquariums. But do you really need all this?

While fancy screen savers do protect your screen from burn in, they also tend to consume large quantities of RAM and processor resources. This reduces the RAM available for your applications and slows down your Macintosh. If you want to get more out of your Macintosh, stick to the basic screen savers or screen saver modules. You'll save money, too.

(By the way, the same goes for many of those fancy Desktop pattern and icon utilities. They eat up RAM and slow things down. If you want your Macintosh to give you all it can, don't fatten it up with window dressing.)

Use Your Monitor's "Built-in" Screen Saver

Every monitor comes with a built-in screen saver. Did you know that? On compact Macintoshes, it's the brightness knob. On freestanding monitors, it's either a brightness knob or a power switch.

When you leave your Macintosh unattended for long periods of time, turn the monitor off or turn the brightness down. This is not only a free way to protect your monitor, but it works extremely well and can save electricity to boot.

Avoid Static Cling

Ever notice how dust seems to cling to the front of your monitor? You could wipe it every day and still come up with a dirty tissue or cloth.

Try wiping it with a used fabric softener cloth like Bounce or Cling Free. This will clear dust off the screen and should prevent dust from settling there as quickly. For a few minutes, it will make your desk area smell nice, too.

Keyboard and Mouse Tricks

If your Macintosh talks to you through your monitor, your keyboard and mouse provide the ways for you to talk back. Here are a few tips for these primary input devices.

Add Extended Keyboard Keys

You've got a standard keyboard or a PowerBook and you want (or need) to be able to use the keys on an extended keyboard. What can you do? You've got two main options:

Why Use a Screen Saver at All? Despite what you might read elsewhere, a screen saver can be an vital piece of software for the health of your monitor. Screen savers usually "blank" out the screen by displaying moving graphic images. This prevents regular screen images—like the menu bar—from "burning in" to the phosphor coating the inside of a screen. If you leave your Macintosh on for more than a few hours a day every day, you should use some sort of screen saver.

♦ Track down a shareware program called *Keyboard Plus* by Berrie Kremers. This program was designed specifically for ISO keyboard and PowerBook users. It installs emulators that give you access to extended keyboard keys, including the numeric keypad.

♦ Use CE Software's *QuicKeys* to add the keys you need. The Alias Keystrokes feature lets you do this. The trick here is to have an extended keyboard attached when adding the keystrokes since this feature of QuicKeys requires that you be able to type in both keys—the desired key and the alias—when assigning the alias.

Use a Mouse Pad

Although a mousepad is not required when using a mouse, it does have two advantages:

♦ A mouse pad usually provides good traction for the mouse.

♦ A mouse pad helps assure that there's sufficient space on your desk surface set aside for using a mouse.

Use a Trackball

If your desk is often so cluttered you can't find room to roll your mouse around (even with a mouse pad claiming territory), it's time to look into a trackball. While a trackball has the same basic parts as a mouse—a rolling ball and a button—it puts the ball on top where you can roll it with your fingers without having to move the whole unit. It may take some getting used to, but it works just as well as a standard mouse.

Miscellaneous Hardware Tricks

Here are a few additional hardware tricks you might find useful.

Power Down Before Plugging In

Always shut off your Macintosh before connecting or disconnecting peripherals. Failing to do so may cause temporary or even permanent damage to your equipment.

At this point you may be shaking your head, thinking about all the times you've plugged in your mouse, keyboard, modem, or printer with your Macintosh turned on. By doing this, you are courting disaster. How long does it take to turn off your computer, plug something in, and turn it back on? Less time that it would take for your Apple dealer to replace a damaged motherboard, SCSI port, or fuse? Why take chances?

Use an A/B Switch

You've got two serial ports on your Macintosh, but three serial devices: a modem, a printer, and a MIDI setup. You're going nuts because every time you need to use the device that isn't plugged in, you need to reach behind your Macintosh and fiddle around with the plugs. Is there a solution? Of course. Get a serial A/B switch.

An A/B switch is a hardware device you can use to manually switch active devices. Plug the A/B switch into one of your serial ports, then plug two devices into the A/B switch. When you want to use one device, turn the knob on the front of the A/B switch box to the appropriate letter (A or B). When you want to use the other, switch to the other letter. Simple, no?

Here are a few things to consider:

♦ An A/B switch does not add serial ports. It only adds the convenience of switching among devices. You can still only use two serial devices at a time.

♦ A/B switches let you plug in two devices. You can also get A/B/C/D switches to plug in four devices. Other configurations are available.

♦ Automatic A/B switches are also available. Most of these use software to set the switch.

♦ If you really need more serial ports (because you need to use more than two serial devices at a time), check into serial port cards manufactured by Creative Solutions, Applied Engineering, and Digiboard.

Install and Use the Programmer's Switch

"The programmer's switch is for people who want to write application programs on the Macintosh IIcx. If you aren't an applications developer, do not install the switch. Installing it and using it incorrectly can result in loss of data."

That's what Apple says about the programmer's switch in the *Macintosh IIcx Owner's Guide*. It makes similar frightening comments in other owner's guides. Don't let Apple scare you. This switch isn't going to cause your computer to self-destruct. What it can do is give you a way to restart the computer without powering it down.

The programmer's switch normally appears as a pair of plastic buttons or tabs on the front or side of your Macintosh CPU. One button, which has a tiny triangle on it, lets you restart your Macintosh. The other button is the programmer's interrupt button, which is commonly used by programmers (like Apple says) for debugging software. Not all Macintosh models have externally accessible programmer's switches. If yours does, it may or may not have been installed by your Apple dealer.

Use the restart button only when your Macintosh is completely frozen and you'd have to power down anyway. Don't press the button unless you really want to restart—your Macintosh won't ask any questions and it won't save any documents first. It'll just restart.

In case you're wondering, the programmer's interrupt button puts a very un-Macintoshlike window on the screen with a greater than symbol in it. A programmer knows what to do with this. If you ever press this button by mistake and find this window staring you in the face, press **G** and then **Return** to go back to whatever document was active. You might consider restarting your Macintosh with the **Restart** command under the **Special** menu afterward just to clear out RAM.

Chapter 7

· ·

Printing Tricks

Printing enables you to share the results of your computing efforts with others. Write a letter, a report, or a shopping list, and print it to take it with you. Draw a picture, lay out a newsletter, or create a financial worksheet, and print it to show it to others. Most of what you do on your computer will end up, sooner or later, on paper. This chapter provides some tips and tricks for helping you get it there.

Output Tricks
· ·

What are you going to print? How are you going to print it? This section provides some tips.

Choose a Printer with the Chooser
If your Macintosh is connected to more than one printer, you can use the **Chooser** to pick the one you want to print to.

1 Choose **Chooser** from the **Apple** menu.

2 On the left side of the **Chooser** window, click on the icon for the type of printer you want to print to.

3 On the right side of the **Chooser** window, click on the name of the printer you want to print to.

4 Close the **Chooser**.

5 A dialog box may appear, warning you that you have made changes and should check the **Page Setup** dialog box in open applications. Click **OK**.

The next time you use the **Print** command, options for the printer you selected appear and the document is printed to that printer.

Choose a Printer with a Keystroke

If you have CE Software's *QuicKeys*, you can use the Choosy extension to choose a printer with a single keystroke, bypassing the Chooser completely. Now Software's *NowMenus* also lets you do this by assigning keystrokes to Chooser options on the hierarchical Apple menu that NowMenus creates.

Print a List of a Folder's Contents

You can print a list of the contents of a folder by choosing **Print Window** from the Finder's **File** menu when that folder's window is active. A standard **Print** dialog box appears; just click **Print** to send the information to your printer. Here are some important points to remember when doing this:

♦ If you are viewing the window in a List view, the printout will include all items in the window, including ones that don't fit in the window on screen. The printout will go to multiple pages if necessary. The item list will be in the same order as the window view and will include all the information shown in the window: kind, size, label, date, etc. In addition, if you're using System 7's outline feature to show multiple folders and their contents in the same window, the outline will also print. This is a great way to show the contents of more than one folder without printing more than one list.

♦ If you are viewing the window in an Icon view, only those icons that appear within the window will print.

Print a Picture of the Screen

Ever need to get a snapshot of your Macintosh screen on paper? In the old days of System 6 and ImageWriter printers, pressing **Command-Shift-4** sent a screen image to the ImageWriter for printing. With System 7 and a laser printer, it takes a bit more work.

1 Press **Command-Shift-3** to activate the built-in FKEY to take a snapshot of your Macintosh screen. You'll hear a camera clicking sound and your mouse will freeze for a moment while the snapshot is being processed.

2 Open your hard disk icon. There should be a TeachText PICT document file there called *Picture 1*.

3 Double-click this file to open it. If you have TeachText 7.0 or later or SimpleText installed on your Macintosh, it will launch and open the file. (If you do not have a current version of TeachText or SimpleText, you'll have to open the file with a graphics application like Claris's *MacDraw Pro* or Deneba's *Canvas*.)

4 Choose **Print** (**Command-P**) from the **File** menu.

5 In the **Standard Print** dialog box that appears, click **Print**.

If you have a large monitor, the image may print on more than one page. To get it all on one page, use the **Page Setup** command under the **File** menu to specify a percentage to reduce the image before printing it.

Print Closer to the Edge of the Paper

Laser printers normally require roughly ½-inch margins all around the edge of a page. Why? So that toner doesn't spill inside the printer. This sets a minimum margin size for your documents, one you might want to override.

You can print closer to the edge of the paper by turning on the **Larger Print Area** check box in the **Print Options** dialog box, as shown in Figure 7.1. Get to the **Print Options** dialog box by clicking

```
┌─────────────────────────────────────────────────────────────┐
│ LaserWriter 8.0 Options                    8.0    ┌─────────┐ │
│                                                   │   OK    │ │
│ ┌──────────────────┐ Visual Effects:             └─────────┘ │
│ │ Paper size in inches│ ☐ Flip Horizontal          ┌─────────┐ │
│ │    Width:  8.5    │ ☐ Flip Vertical            │ Cancel  │ │
│ │    Height: 11     │ ☐ Invert Image             └─────────┘ │
│ │                   │                            · · · · · · │
│ │ Margins in inches │ Printer Options:            ┌─────────┐ │
│ │    Top:    0.111  │ ☒ Substitute Fonts          │  Help   │ │
│ │    Left:   0.25   │ ☒ Smooth Text               └─────────┘ │
│ │    Bottom: 0.111  │ ☒ Smooth Graphics                       │
│ │    Right:  0.25   │ ☐ Precision Bitmap Alignment (4% reduction)│
│ └──────────────────┘ ☒ Larger Print Area (Fewer Downloadable Fonts)│
│                      ☐ Unlimited Downloadable Fonts in a Document│
└─────────────────────────────────────────────────────────────┘
```

Figure 7.1 Print Options lets you change a number of printing options on laser printers.

Options in either the **Page Setup** or **Print** dialog box. If you click on the dog/cow sample illustration, you can display the actual margins which will be used by the printer. This is also shown in Figure 7.1.

Disable Font Substitution

System 7 comes with TrueType versions of the standard Macintosh fonts: Geneva, New York, and Monaco. If you want to print these fonts on a PostScript printer, be sure to turn **Font Substitution** off in the **Print** or **Print Options** dialog box (see Figure 7.1). This option is turned on automatically. If you leave **Font Substitution** on, your Macintosh will substitute Helvetica, Times, and Courier fonts, respectively.

Automation Tricks

· ·

If you'd like to see your documents printed automatically, don't skip over this section. In it, you'll find some tips for unattended printing.

Print Batches of Files

You've got a folder full of files created with different applications. You need to print them all. Do you start opening them, one by one, and use the Print command for each? There's a better way.

Which Font Is Used to Print? With bitmapped, TrueType, and PostScript fonts installed in your Macintosh, you may wonder which font is actually used to print on a PostScript printer. If a required font is not included in the printer's ROM, your Macintosh looks for fonts to send to it in the following order:

- PostScript
- TrueType
- Bitmapped (scaled)

If you've got a QuickDraw printer like an ImageWriter, a StyleWriter, or a LaserWriter IIsc, PostScript fonts aren't understood by the printer at all. In that case, your Macintosh looks for fonts to send to the printer in this order:

- TrueType
- PostScript (processed with *ATM*—if *ATM* is installed)
- Bitmapped (scaled)

1 Select the icons for the files you want printed. If the files are in multiple folders, use the List view outline feature of System 7 to see the contents of all the folders. Remember to hold down the Shift key while clicking each icon to select them all.

2 Choose **Print** (**Command-P**) from the Finder's **File** menu.

3 Your Macintosh begins launching applications and displaying **Print** dialog boxes for each one. Click **Print** in each dialog box that appears. Each application will display only one **Print** dialog box no matter how many of its documents were included in the selection. After an application sends information to the printer, it automatically quits.

If your Macintosh attempts to open more applications than available RAM allows, it might display an error message. It may also display an error message if there isn't enough RAM available to launch PrintMonitor and print. For this reason, it's a good idea to limit the number of different kinds of documents you print in a batch. You should have no problems if you choose several documents in only one or two applications.

Delay Printing

You can use PrintMonitor (or another print spooler application) to delay printing. For this to work, Background Printing must be turned on in the Chooser for the printer you plan to print to.

1 Open the document that you want to print later.

2 Choose **Print** (**Command-P**) from the **File** menu.

3 Make any necessary changes to the default settings in the standard **Print** dialog box and click the **Print** button.

4 The application displays a "Printing" message and sends the document to PrintMonitor. Wait until the "Printing" message disappears and then choose **PrintMonitor** from the System 7 **Application** menu. It may take a little while for PrintMonitor to appear on the menu, so if you pull down the **Application** menu immediately and don't see it, release the menu, wait a moment, and try again.

5 The PrintMonitor window appears. It lists all the documents currently waiting to be printed. Make sure the name of the document you want to print later is selected in the PrintMonitor window and click **Set Print Time**.

6 A dialog box like the one in Figure 7.2 appears. Use it to set the time (and, if desired, the date) that you want the selected document to print. Then click **OK**.

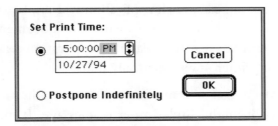

Figure 7.2 Set the printing time and date with PrintMonitor.

7 Back in the PrintMonitor window, a suitcase icon appears before the document name. The print time and date also appears. This is illustrated in Figure 7.3.

8 To go back to work, choose another application from the Application menu. PrintMonitor should close automatically.

Repeat these steps for as many documents as you like. The documents you set to print later will automatically print at the specified time as long as the printer is properly connected and ready. Use this to print documents you don't need right away, leaving your printer free to print documents you need now.

Canceling a Print Job

Once you've sent something to PrintMonitor for printing, you can cancel it at any time.

1 Choose **PrintMonitor** from the System 7 **Application** menu.

2 In the list of documents to be printed, click the name of the document you want to cancel.

3 If the document is in the **Printing** edit box, click **Cancel Printing**. If the document is in the **Waiting** list, click **Remove from List**. After a moment, the item disappears.

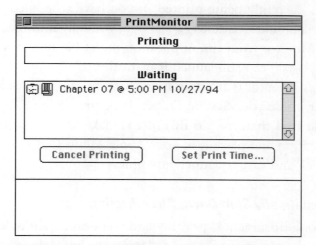

Figure 7.3 PrintMonitor's window displays the scheduled printing time and date for documents to be printed later.

PrintMonitor

PrintMonitor is the print spooling application that's part of the System software. It makes it possible to have your System 7 or System 6 MultiFinder Macintosh print in the background, freeing up your Macintosh to do other things.

While perfectionists might argue that PrintMonitor has many flaws, it's got two main things going for it: It works and it's free. If you find that PrintMonitor doesn't offer all the features you need in a print spooler, check out Fifth Generation Systems' *SuperLaserSpool* which offers all the features of PrintMonitor and then some.

4 Repeat for as many documents as you need to.

5 To go back to work, choose another application from the **Application** menu. PrintMonitor should close automatically.

If a document is already being printed when you cancel it, several pages may print before it is finally removed from the PrintMonitor window.

Launch PrintMonitor Manually

PrintMonitor only appears on the Application menu if there are documents currently being printed. If you have scheduled all documents to print later and decide to cancel one, you may find that you can't access PrintMonitor from the Application menu because it isn't active. Don't worry—you can still launch it manually.

PrintMonitor is an application that you can find inside the Extensions folder inside your System Folder. Launch it by double-clicking its icon. If you find that you do this often, make an alias of the PrintMonitor application and place it in your Apple Menu Items folder. That'll make it quick and easy to launch any time.

Automatically Shut Down After Printing

If a long document is printing and you don't want to wait around for it to finish, you can make your Macintosh shut down automatically when it's done. Simply select **Shut Down** from the Finder's Special menu. A dialog box like the one in Figure 7.4 appears, warning you that a

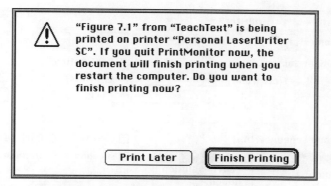

Figure 7.4 PrintMonitor displays this dialog
box if you Shut Down while a document is
being printed.

document is being printed. Click **Finish Printing**. Your Macintosh
prints the entire document and then shuts down.

Resource Saving Tricks

Printing is probably one of the most wasteful aspects of computing. After all, it takes time, toner or ink, and paper. In this section, you'll find
some tips for saving these resources when you print.

Save Time

While it's true that you don't have to "baby-sit" a printer while it prints,
you have to admit that printing can be, at times, painfully slow. Here
are a few tips for speeding things up.

- ♦ When printing on a laser printer, choose **Black & White** in the
  Print dialog box whenever possible. This will force any colors
  in the document to change to either black or white—not much
  of a problem if your document is already in black and white.
  Choosing **Grayscale/Color** can slow down the printing process
  unnecessarily.

- ♦ Some print dialog boxes (like QuarkXPress's, which is shown in
  Figure 7.5) offer different quality outputs. Choosing something
  less than best quality will speed the printout considerably. The

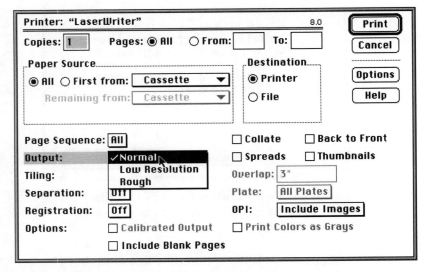

Figure 7.5 QuarkXPress offers different output options, some faster than others.

document that emerges from your printer will not be camera-ready, but it should be fine as a first draft.

♦ When printing on an ImageWriter, choose **Draft** or **Faster** in the **Print** dialog box whenever possible. Draft doesn't use the fonts you specified, but gets all the text on paper for proofreading and the like. Faster uses the correct fonts but doesn't print as dark or as clearly as Best.

Save Ink and Toner

The tips for faster printing above can also save ink or toner. Here are a few more tips for saving the black stuff:

♦ When printing draft documents, remove any heavy black graphics (or set them so that they don't print) before choosing the **Print** (**Command-P**) command.

♦ When your laser printer displays the low toner indicator, shut off the printer, remove the toner cartridge, and *gently* rock it back and forth. Replace the cartridge and turn the printer back on. The rocking motion may be enough to settle the toner evenly in the cartridge, letting you print up to a few hundred more pages of text.

A Word About Recycled Toner Cartridges

Recycling is great. It helps us reuse valuable resources and minimize landfills. This is especially important for waste products that are not biodegradable, like toner cartridges.

Many office supply stores sell recycled toner cartridges. These are used cartridges that have been refilled with toner. They're generally $10 to $30 cheaper than brand new toner cartridges, making them seem like a real money-saver.

Unfortunately, as toner cartridges are used, they can become damaged. Print quality can be affected, depending on the damage. A scratch on a roller, for example, can leave a line on every single sheet of paper you print. Since the damage is in the cartridge itself, there's usually nothing you can do about it.

If you do use recycled toner cartridges, keep an eye out for stray marks on your documents. If you find that the quality of the printouts isn't up to par for final documents, remove it. Don't throw it out, though. In a work environment with many laser printers, you might be able to use a damaged cartridge on a printer normally used for draft or internally circulated documents. Otherwise, it might make a good spare for emergencies.

♦ Check out a program called *Toner Tuner* by Working Software, Inc. This program works with your printer driver to reduce the amount of toner or ink your printer uses by letting you control the darkness of the print. It works with most PostScript and non-PostScript printers, including laser, dot matrix, and inkjet printers.

Save Trees

With hundreds or thousands of acres of forest being cut down every day to meet the paper demands of today's businesses, you should try to do your part to minimize paper waste. Here are some tips:

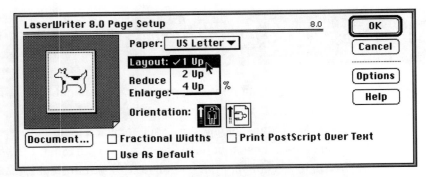

Figure 7.6 The LaserWriter 8.0 print driver offers multiple page printing on one page.

♦ Save unneeded documents that are printed on only one side. Use the unprinted side for printing other draft documents or cut the sheets in half or quarters and use them for scrap note paper.

♦ If your application or **Page Setup** dialog box offers it, print multiple pages of a draft document on one page. The LaserWriter 8.0 printer driver offers 1 Up, 2 Up, or 4 Up printing, as shown in Figure 7.6.

♦ Recycle used paper. Even if this is not mandatory in your area of the country, imagine how much less waste there would be if *everyone* recycled!

Chapter 8

· ·

Mobile Slick Tricks

With the release of the original Macintosh Portable, Macintosh computing "went mobile." Years later, the PowerBooks and PowerBook Duos gave Apple a strong presence in the notebook computer market. Today, PowerBooks remain among the top-selling notebook computers in the world. It doesn't seem possible to take a plane anywhere these days without seeing one on someone's tray table during the flight.

The Newton, which debuted at MacWorld Boston 1993, made Apple computing even easier to take along. While it is not a Macintosh, with the help of the Newton Connection Kit, a Newton has no trouble communicating with one—or with an IBM-compatible machine running Microsoft Windows, if it has to. Before long, you'll be seeing Newtons in your doctor's office, at business meetings, and on golf courses—if you golf, of course.

This chapter offers some tips and tricks for the desktop Macintosh's slimmer and trimmer sibling, as well as its pocket-sized cousin. If you're fortunate enough to have one of these computing devices, this chapter is for you.

PowerBook Tricks

PowerBook users have all the power of a desktop Macintosh in a portable package. But with that package comes new concerns: battery conservation, connectivity, and file synchronization. This section provides a few tricks for dealing with them.

Monitor Battery Power

The Battery desk accessory, which is part of the System software for PowerBooks, enables you to check battery power and put your Power-Book to sleep (more on sleep in a moment).

1. Choose **Battery** from the Apple menu.

2. The Battery DA appears. It can be either expanded (as shown in Figure 8.1) or collapsed. Use the tiny "handle" at the far right side of the desk accessory to expand or collapse it.

3. Solid black boxes indicate the battery level. A **System Sleep** button lets you put the PowerBook to sleep.

4. Click the close box to close the Battery DA.

Put Your PowerBook to Sleep

When you put your PowerBook to sleep, you're saving almost as much power as you do when you shut it down. In the so-called "sleep state," your PowerBook uses very little power. In fact, it can remain sleeping on battery power for days. The benefit of putting your PowerBook to sleep rather than shutting it down is that the contents of RAM are not lost. Your Macintosh can wake quickly, too—much more quickly than it starts.

Under System 7.0.x, there are two separate kinds of sleep that you can control separately: System sleep and internal drive sleep. Under

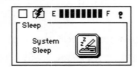

Figure 8.1 The Battery
desk accessory

System 7.1.x, there is only one kind of sleep which covers both the system and the internal drive. Put your PowerBook to sleep with the Sleep command under the Special menu or the Battery desk accessory. Set sleep options with the PowerBook control panel.

Putting Your Internal Drive to Sleep

 If you're using System 7.0.x and have the ability to set the internal drive sleep period, don't set it for too short a period. Waking a hard disk consumes a lot of power. If you're using an application that frequently consults or saves to the internal hard disk you could burn up a significant amount of battery power each time the hard disk wakes.

Use the PowerBook Control Panel

The PowerBook control panel, which is illustrated in Figure 8.2, lets you configure how your PowerBook tries to conserve power as it runs.

1 Launch the **PowerBook** control panel.

2 Use the sliding bar to set how your PowerBook runs. **Maximum Performance** increases PowerBook reaction time and speed while reducing battery conservation. **Maximum Conservation** saves power but decreases performance.

3 If desired, click the **Options** button. The **Battery Conservation Options** dialog box, which is illustrated in Figure 8.3, appears. Use the check box and radio buttons to specify exactly how you want your PowerBook to conserve battery power. When you're finished, click **OK** to accept your settings.

4 Click the close box to close the **PowerBook** control panel.

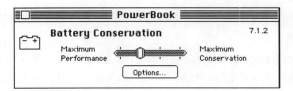

Figure 8.2 The PowerBook control panel

```
┌─────────────────────────────────────────┐
│  ┌─+┐  Battery Conservation Options      │
│  └───┘                                   │
│  ········································· │
│      ☐ Don't sleep when plugged in       │
│  ········································· │
│  Processor Cycling                       │
│      ◉ Allow cycling (more battery savings) │
│      ○ Don't allow cycling               │
│  ········································· │
│  Processor Speed                         │
│      ◉ Standard speed                    │
│      ○ Reduced speed (more battery savings) │
│  ········································· │
│                                          │
│  ( Use Defaults )    (( Cancel ))  ( OK ) │
└─────────────────────────────────────────┘
```

Figure 8.3 Battery conservation options offered by the PowerBook control panel

Use a RAM Disk

As with any computer, motorized parts consume a lot of power. PowerBooks have two such parts: the hard disk and the floppy disk. While you may not notice how often the hard disk in a desktop Macintosh spins as you work, it's quite noticeable in a PowerBook. Each spin consumes power. If the PowerBook is running on battery power, each spin means less running time.

A RAM disk is the best solution for this problem. A RAM disk, which was discussed in Chapter 3, enables you to use RAM as disk space. Because RAM doesn't need a motor to work, it uses much less power than a hard or floppy disk drive. It also has the added benefit of being faster than a hard disk.

PowerBooks come with a RAM disk utility built into the Memory control panel, which was also discussed in Chapter 3. Figure 8.4 shows what it looks like. Here's how to use it to create a RAM disk.

1 Open the **Memory** control panel.

2 Click the **On** radio button in the **RAM Disk** section of the dialog box.

3 Drag the sliding bar to set the size of the RAM disk. Fifty percent of available RAM is usually enough on a PowerBook with 8 MB or more of RAM installed.

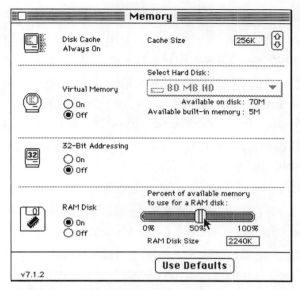

Figure 8.4 The Memory control panel on a
PowerBook

4 Click the close box to close the **Memory** control panel and
choose Restart from the Special menu.

The RAM disk appears as an icon on your desktop when you restart.
You can copy any files you like to the RAM disk, including large applications and files that don't completely load when launched. This can
greatly reduce hard disk access while working with these files.

RAM Disk Contents Can Be Lost!

 A RAM disk is not the same a regular disk. When you shut down your
Macintosh or it bombs, causing you to restart, the contents of a
RAM disk are lost! This applies to all Macintosh models except the
PowerBook 100, which uses battery power to retain RAM disk con-
tents even when the computer is turned off. For more information
about RAM disk danger and how you can avoid it, be sure to consult
Chapter 3.

Start Your Macintosh from a RAM Disk

Since your Macintosh accesses System files periodically while you work, it's a good idea to use a RAM disk as your Startup disk. Here's how.

1 Trim down your System folder so it contains only the files you absolutely need for your work. To do this, remove any unneeded fonts, desk accessories, control panels, and extensions.

2 Create a large RAM disk. It must be at least large enough to hold the System folder.

3 Drag your System folder icon to the RAM disk icon to copy it.

4 Open the **Startup Disk** control panel. Choose the RAM disk as your startup disk. Close the **Startup Disk** control panel.

5 Choose **Restart** from the **Special** menu. When your Power-Book restarts, it'll start from the RAM disk.

If you have a large enough RAM disk, you can copy applications and documents to the RAM disk as well. This will further reduce disk access. If you put your PowerBook to sleep rather than shut it down, you can retain the contents of the RAM disk. Otherwise, each time you shut down your PowerBook, you'll have to repeat Steps 3 through 5 to run from the RAM disk again.

One important thing to remember when doing this: Since the contents of your System folder can change while you work, be sure to copy changed files from your System folder back to your hard disk before shutting down. This way the most recent versions of preferences and settings files are stored on your hard disk where they're not easily lost.

Turn Down Brightness

Backlit PowerBook screens are also big consumers of power. You can decrease the amount of power your PowerBook's screen uses by using the PowerBook Display control panel to dim the screen when the PowerBook is idle. This is like a built-in screen saver for the PowerBook. As soon as you begin using your PowerBook again, the screen image comes back.

Be Sure to Set Screen Dimming

 Even if your PowerBook is connected to an external power source, it's a good idea to use the PowerBook Display control panel to dim the screen. If the screen is left on for an extended period of time, it can become temporarily damaged by the image left there.

Run Down the Battery

PowerBook batteries, like many other rechargeable batteries, have a memory. If the battery isn't completely drained before it is recharged, after a while it "thinks" it doesn't *need* to be completely drained before it is recharged. The result: reduced battery life.

It's a good idea to completely run down your PowerBook's battery prior to recharging it as often as possible. You can purchase a discharging device to help you do this if you don't want to leave your PowerBook on—check your computer reseller for options. (By the way, this principle applies to the batteries on cellular phones and video cameras, as well.)

Note: This does not apply to the Powerbook 500 series computers' "Intelligent Battery."

Connect to a Desktop Macintosh with File Sharing

System 7 file sharing offers an easy way to connect your PowerBook to a desktop Macintosh. Use AppleTalk connectors to physically connect the two machines, then use file sharing to set up the network and access one computer's disks from the other's.

1. Use the **Sharing Setup** control panel to identify each Macintosh's **Owner, Password,** and **Name**.

2. Use the **User & Groups** control panel to create user accounts and set privileges.

3. Select the disks or folders you want to share and use the **File** menu's **Sharing** command to make it accessible over the network.

4. Use the **Sharing Setup** control panel to turn file sharing on or off.

File Synchronization Software With the widespread use of PowerBooks, software developers have been quick to meet file synchronization needs. *PowerMerge* by Leader Technologies and *Inline Sync* by Inline Design/Microseeds Publishing are just two of the products that perform this function. Other PowerBook utility packages may include their own synchronization software. This software can save a lot of time and effort by making it easy to find and update both your computers with the latest version of any changed file.

⑤ Use the **Chooser** to mount a shared volume over the network.

Once you mount your PowerBook's hard disk on your desktop Macintosh, you can access any of the files on it as defined by the privileges you set. If you prefer, you can mount your desktop Macintosh's hard disk on your PowerBook. In fact, you can do both at the same time if you like.

Use AppleTalk Remote Access

AppleTalk Remote Access, or ARA, was discussed in Chapter 6. You can use this program, which comes with PowerBooks, to use file sharing over a modem connection. This makes it possible to access your desktop Macintosh from your PowerBook from anywhere in the world.

Synchronize Files

You've got a desktop Macintosh and a PowerBook. You keep certain files on both machines. How do you make sure the most up-to-date file is on both of them? The answer: Synchronize. Here are a few tricks for making file synchronization easier.

♦ Copy files from your desktop Macintosh to your PowerBook before taking your PowerBook on the road. Copy files from your PowerBook to your desktop Macintosh when you return. This will be effective only if you do it consistently and only use one computer at a time.

Quick Quiz: Macintosh on Television

Name a current and wildly popular network sitcom where you can see a Macintosh computer on the main character's desk. Know the answer? Know what kind of Macintosh it is? How about the Macintosh that occupied the same spot in the 1992/1993 season?

The answer is NBC's *Seinfeld*. Jerry has a Macintosh Duo with Duo-Dock and color monitor on his desk. In the first few seasons of *Seinfeld*, Jerry had a compact Macintosh.

What other popular network sitcom, which is now in syndication, featured a Macintosh computer on one of its character's desks? What model was that?

It's another NBC show: *Night Court*. Judge Harry Stone also had a compact Macintosh on his desk.

♦ Store all files that are kept on both computers in a separate folder on each machine. This makes it easy to simply open the folders and compare dates.

♦ Use the Finder's **Find** (**Command-F**) command to find files modified since the last time you synchronized. Then compare the dates and copy the files as necessary to update each machine.

♦ Use file synchronization software to simplify or automate the synchronization task.

Newton Tricks

You saw it and you had to have it: a Newton. If you're like other Newton owners, your opinion of Newton probably falls between these two extremes: 1) The Newton is one of the most useful computing tools you've ever used and you wonder how you lived without it, or 2) the Newton is a cute toy but you can't figure out what to *do* with it. The handful of tips and tricks in this section should help point you in the right direction if you're lost in Newtonland.

Improve Handwriting Recognition

One of the biggest complaints new Newton users have is Newton's less than perfect handwriting recognition. Here are a few tips for helping Newton to read your handwriting.

♦ Write with large, clear, well-formed letters. Large characters are easiest for Newton to understand.

♦ Show your Newton the correct word when it doesn't choose the right one. To do this, double-tap the word your Newton came up with to display a list of words it considered. If the correct word is on the list, tap it to replace the incorrect word. This not only corrects the entry, but it helps the Newton to learn how you write that particular word.

♦ Change the Handwriting Style so that it transforms handwriting less quickly. To do this, tap **Extras**, tap **Prefs**, and then tap **Handwriting Style**. Slide the indicator a bit to the right.

♦ When writing, don't rest your hand or fingers on the screen. This may confuse your Newton, which doesn't know whether it should interpret the pressure as part of the information you are entering.

♦ Be sure to put your Newton in Guest mode when letting someone else give it a try. To do this, tap **Extras**, tap **Prefs**, and then tap **Handwriting Style**. Turn on the box for **Configure for Guest User**. When the "guest" has finished, be sure to turn Guest mode off so your Newton can continue to learn from you.

Have Patience

Don't get frustrated when your Newton can't seem to learn how to read your handwriting. It takes time, effort, and patience. If you follow the instructions that came with your Newton and write as clearly as possible, you should see positive results within a reasonable time.

Read Your Own Handwriting

If you don't have the time or patience to teach your Newton how to read your handwriting, turn character recognition off and just write. After all, you can read your handwriting, can't you? This is most useful for jotting down little reminders and notes that don't need to be stored as regular computer data.

Synchronize

The Newton Connection Kit (version 2.0) lets you back up your Newton to a desktop Macintosh with its synchronize function. This function is good for a few tricks:

♦ Use Synchronize to back up the contents of your Newton to a desktop Macintosh. After the first synchronization, three files are maintained: Newton, Backup File, and Archive file. Newton contains the contents of your Newton. Backup File contains the contents of your Newton the last time you synchronized. Archive File contains the items removed from your Newton each time you synchronize.

♦ Use Synchronize to restore the Newton file to your Newton in the event of a Newton data loss.

♦ Use **Copy** and **Paste** on your Macintosh to copy items from the Archive file to the Newton file. Then use Synchronize to get the old information back onto your Newton.

♦ Since the Newton Connection Kit "recreates" Newton's resident applications on your Macintosh, you can enter data on your Macintosh and use Synchronize to get it into your Newton.

Try Shareware

Shareware, or "try-before-you-buy" software, has been available for desktop computers for years. You may not realize it, but there is Newton shareware around as well. You can find it on many online services and BBSes. With shareware prices ranging from free or a simple postcard up to about $20, shareware can be an excellent value. One thing to keep in mind, however: To install Newton shareware that you obtain on a Macintosh disk, you'll need the Newton Connection Kit.

Connect with NewtonMail

NewtonMail is a service of Apple Computer, Inc. To use it, you need a NewtonMail account, a Newton, and a Newton fax modem. Once set

Quick Quiz: Newton in the Funny Papers

Name a popular comic strip that featured the Newton not long after it was first released. Which character had one?

The answer is Gary Trudeau's Michael Doonesbury in the comic strip *Doonesbury*.

up, you can use Newton mail to exchange NewtonMail messages with other Newton users, and any electronic mail system that can be accessed through the Internet. (For more information about connecting through the Internet, be sure to check out Chapter 5.)

Display Newton Easter Eggs

An Easter Egg is a hidden message or graphic placed inside a computer's software or ROMs by a programmer. There are hundreds of Macintosh Easter Eggs—you can find them sprinkled throughout this book. Here are a few just for Newton.

- To find out where Elvis was last sighted, tap **Find**, write Elvis, and tap the **Close** button on the keyboard. Before the keyboard disappears, it asks, "Add Elvis to word list?" Answer **Yes** or **No**. Then tap **All**.

- To see a list of the Apple developers who created Newton, tap **Assist**, write About Newton in the **Please** field, and tap **Do**.

- To see a special graphic when you turn on your Newton, tap **Extras**, tap **Prefs**, and tap **Personal**. Double-tap the **Country** field. When the keyboard appears, type Graceland. Tap the **Close** button on the keyboard. Before it disappears, it asks, "Add Graceland to word list?" Answer **Yes** or **No**. Close **Preferences**, close **Extras**, and turn your Newton off. When you turn your Newton back on, you'll get a new greeting.

Chapter 9

Maintenance and Troubleshooting Tricks

An ounce of prevention is worth a pound of cure. Whoever first made that statement may have owned a computer because it certainly can be applied to computer equipment. It's amazing how a few simple maintenance tasks and protective measures can help keep your Macintosh running smoothly for years.

In this chapter, you'll learn some tips for taking care of your hardware investment. Because good maintenance isn't always enough, however, this chapter will also provide a bunch of tips and tricks for figuring out what's wrong—and fixing the problem—when your Macintosh is feeling under the weather.

Power Protection Tricks

Power level fluctuations, which are called spikes, surges, and brownouts, can do serious damage to computer components. Here are some ways you can protect against these power problems.

Use a Surge Suppresser

A surge suppresser is a device that plugs into the wall socket and usually offers two to eight plugs to provide power to multiple computer or electronics devices. Surge suppressers have fuses and often have their own separate power switches that add even more protection. No computer should be plugged directly into a wall socket!

Use a UPS

An uninterrupted power supply (UPS) is most commonly used to prevent systems from shutting down in the event of a power outage. Many UPS units, however, also filter incoming power to provide smooth power levels for devices plugged into them. While more expensive than a standard surge suppresser, you've got the added benefit of being able to continue working even in the event of short-term power failures.

Use a Telephone Surge Suppresser

Your local power company and its electrical lines aren't the only source of power hazards. If you use a modem or fax modem, it can be damaged by phone line power problems. Telephone line surge suppressers, which are often included on regular surge suppressers, help protect against phone line power fluctuations. Use a standard phone cable to connect the suppresser to the wall jack. Then use another standard cable to connect the suppresser to the modem or fax modem. (By the way, this can help protect regular fax machines, too.)

Power Down During Thunderstorms

If you live in an area prone to thunderstorms, consider shutting down your computer equipment during storms, especially violent ones. Lightning strikes on or near power or phone lines can cause the kinds of spikes and surges that you buy surge suppressers to protect against. If the strike is close enough, however, no surge suppresser is going to stop its power.

Virus Protection Tricks

Computer viruses are possibly one of the most frightening hazards for computer users. If you follow a few simple precautions, however, you can keep your computer free of viruses and the damage they cause.

Use Anti-Viral Software

Anti-viral software is your first defense against computer viruses. These software products can perform any or all of the following functions:

♦ Protect against virus infections. Many anti-viral software products work constantly to check your system for indications of virus activity. If you insert an infected floppy disk, for example, this software will spot the virus and alert you before the virus has a chance to infect your system. These anti-viral products usually contain a System extension or control panel or both so that they load as soon as you start your Macintosh.

♦ Detect virus infections. Many anti-viral software products include a scan function you can use to search disks for infected files. If the software finds an infected file, it alerts you immediately so you can act to remove it. Virus detection scanners usually work as applications that you launch manually and put to work.

♦ Remove infections or infected files. Once a virus is detected, many anti-viral software products have the ability to remove infected files. Not all viruses can be removed by anti-viral software, however. Most anti-viral software provides instructions on how you can remove a virus if it can't. Sometimes the solution is as easy as rebuilding your Desktop file.

Update Anti-Viral Software Regularly

Each time a new virus comes to light, chances are your existing anti-viral software won't be able to detect it. That means that it's *vital* that you keep your anti-viral software up to date. If possible, watch for news of new viruses in Macintosh magazines like *MacWEEK*, *MacUser*, and *MacWorld*. When you read about one, get the update to your anti-viral

Disinfectant

Not everyone has a lot of money to spend on anti-viral software, updates, and update services. If you're on a tight budget, check out *Disinfectant* by John Norstad. It is updated each time a new virus is discovered—updates are always available within days of the discovery. Disinfectant includes an extension that can identify infected floppy disks as they are inserted. Its application can scan or disinfect disks, folders, or specific files.

It's online help feature includes an extensive virus reference material that'll teach you everything you need to know about Macintosh viruses. Disinfectant is widely available on online services and BBSes. Perhaps best of all, this little gem is free.

software—it's normally available within days of the discovery of a new virus. If the maker of the anti-viral software you use offers an update service, sign up for it. There might be a fee involved, but paying that small fee might save your files one day.

Lock Floppy Disks

As mentioned in Chapter 6, one surefire way to protect floppy disks from infection is to lock them. When a disk is locked, nothing can be written to it. That means nothing can be changed—which means a virus cannot infect the disk. It's as simple as that.

Be sure to lock all original program disks and other disks containing information you don't need to change. This will protect the disk from viruses better than any other method.

Spread the Word—Not the Virus

If you find a virus on your system, don't keep it a secret. There's a chance that any disk inserted into your computer since the last time you checked for viruses may also be infected. Tell anyone who may have a disk that has been in your system. This will help prevent the further spread of the virus.

Cleanup Tricks

A dirty Macintosh isn't only unattractive; it might have trouble operating. Here are some tips for keeping your Macintosh clean.

Don't Smoke

Secondary smoke can be harmful to your computer's health, too. If you're a smoker, do your Macintosh a favor and don't smoke near it. Smoke particles find their way inside components and cling to surfaces. Smoke on the magnetic surface of a floppy disk can cause data access errors.

Blow the Dust Out of Your CPU

Periodically open your CPU and blow out the dust that might have accumulated. Dust buildup leads to heat buildup which can permanently damage computer components. When blowing out dust, it's best to use compressed air that comes in a can. You can find it in most office or computer supply stores.

Use a Dust Cover

If you work in a dusty environment, invest in computer covers to keep the dust out of your equipment when you're not using it.

Clean Floppy Drives

Clean your floppy disk drive(s) regularly—at least a few times a year. This keeps the heads free of dirt and dust that can corrupt data on floppy disks.

A number of companies make floppy disk drive cleaners. These normally consist of a special floppy disk with a hard cloth insert instead of magnetic media and some kind of cleaning fluid. 3M makes drive cleaners with treated inserts. Other companies, like Allsop, make reusable inserts and provide a plastic bottle of fluid you can drop onto the insert before using it. Either way, when you insert the special disk into your drive, your Macintosh tries to read it. As it tries, its heads get cleaned. When it reports that the disk cannot be read and it offers to initialize it, click Eject to remove the disk.

Use a Keyboard "Skin"

Dust and humidity are two environmental hazards that can prevent a keyboard from working properly. A thin plastic covering designed specifically to mold to the keys on your keyboard can protect it from both of these elements. You'll hate it right after you install it, but after about a week or so, you won't even notice it. If you've ever taken apart an extended keyboard and cleaned every single key by hand, you'll realize the value of this simple protective device.

Keep Your Mouse Territory Clean

As your mouse rolls around your desk surface or mouse pad, it picks up whatever dust, crumbs, other debris might be in its path. These particles accumulate inside the mouse and can cause it to malfunction. Keep your desk clean to avoid mouse problems. If problems do occur, simply remove the ball in the belly of the mouse, blow out the debris, and replace the ball.

Clean the Plastic Parts

To clean the outer plastic parts of your Macintosh, use a soft cloth and a nonabrasive cleaner. Fantastik is very effective. Don't spray the cleaner directly onto your Macintosh. Instead, spray it on the cloth. You may want to rinse the cleaned components with clear water on a fresh cloth to finish the job.

Desktop File Tricks

Rebuilding the Desktop is a simple software maintenance technique that can prevent missing or incorrect icons and some disk-related errors. Do it once every few months. In this section, you'll learn how.

Rebuild a Floppy Disk's Desktop

To rebuild the Desktop on a floppy disk, follow these steps:

1. Hold down **Command-Option** while inserting the disk.
2. A dialog box like the one in Figure 9.1 appears. Click **OK**.

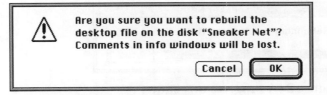

Figure 9.1 Rebuild the Desktop?

❸ A progress box appears like the one in Figure 9.2 appears. It shouldn't take more than a few seconds to rebuild the Desktop on a floppy since it usually contains few files. When the progress box disappears, you can continue working.

Rebuilding the Desktop Erases Get Info Comments

 When you rebuild the Desktop, any comments you may have entered into the Get Info window for a file will be lost. If you want to enter permanent comments in the Get Info window, include them in a file's vers resource—you can find instructions for this in Chapter 10.

About the Desktop

As your work with your Macintosh, it builds and maintains an invisible file (or pair of files) called the Desktop file which it uses to store references to icons and file path information. Your Macintosh uses this information to display icons in the Finder. On a System 7 Macintosh's hard disk, the Desktop file really consists of two invisible files: Desktop DB and Desktop DF. On a System 6 Macintosh's hard disk or on any floppy disk, no matter what version of the System software is running, there's just one invisible file: Desktop.

When your Macintosh experiences system bombs, power outages, and other disruptive events, the Desktop file can become corrupted. Rebuilding the Desktop creates a brand new Desktop file from scratch, eliminating any problems that might otherwise occur.

Figure 9.2 A progress box shows reconstruction in progress.

Rebuild Your Hard Disk's Desktop

To rebuild the Desktop on a hard disk, follow these steps.

1 Hold down **Command-Option** while restarting (or starting) your Macintosh. Keep the keys held down throughout the entire startup process. You may notice that some extensions and control panels that normally appear across the bottom of your startup screen display with X's over them. This is because pressing one or both of these keys may disable those programs.

2 A dialog box like the one in Figure 9.1 appears. Click **OK**.

3 A progress box appears like the one in Figure 9.2 appears. The larger the hard disk and the more files on it, the longer the rebuilding process will take. When the progress box disappears, you can continue working.

If you have multiple hard disks connected to your Macintosh, a dialog box like the one in Figure 9.1 will appear for each one. Click **OK** or **Cancel**, whichever is appropriate.

Rebuild the Desktop Without Restarting

Although it isn't really a good practice, you can rebuild the Desktop of your hard disk without restarting your Macintosh. Here's how:

1 With the **Finder** active, press **Command-Option-Esc**.

2 A dialog box appears, asking if you want to force-quit the Finder. Press **Command-Option** and click **Force Quit**.

3 A dialog box like the one in Figure 9.1 appears. Click **OK**.

4 A progress box like the one in Figure 9.2 appears. When it disappears, you can continue working.

Why isn't it a good idea to rebuild the Desktop like this? Because force-quitting the Finder can corrupt RAM and cause problems later in the work session. It's always a good idea to restart your Macintosh after force-quitting a program. If you have to restart anyway, why not just rebuild the Desktop then?

Miscellaneous Maintenance Tricks

Here are a few other maintenance tips you should consider. All of these will help your Macintosh run trouble-free.

Use Disk Diagnosis or Repair Software

Disk diagnosis or repair software can not only fix major disk problems, it can also fix minor ones, thus preventing major problems from occurring. The "Disk Diagnosis and Repair Software Tricks" section of this chapter discusses a number of useful software packages, including two you might already have.

Reformat Your Hard Disk

Although time consuming to do, reformatting your hard disk is a good way to keep it running smoothly. The formatting and initialization process wipes the disk clean, realigning the magnetic particles on the disk surfaces. It removes any corruption and lets you start fresh. It also gives you an opportunity to add or remove disk partitions to change your filing strategy. Formatting and partitioning a hard disk was discussed in Chapter 6.

Startup Troubleshooting Tricks

When your Macintosh won't start, it's frustrating if you don't know how to deal with it. In this section, you'll find some basic troubleshooting tricks that may help you get your Macintosh started when it seems to want to take the day off.

Check the Batteries

You tried to start your Macintosh IIfx but nothing happened. Everything is properly connected but the darn thing seems dead. What do you do?

Macintosh II, IIx, and IIfx computers use the battery to keep a capacitor inside the computer charged (among other things). This capacitor is what starts the computer when you touch the startup key. If the battery is dead or extremely weak, these computers will appear dead.

Of course, the problem could be worse. A dead Macintosh could indeed be a dead Macintosh. Some more serious problems to check for include a bad power supply or ROM problem.

Translate Weird Startup Sounds

You started your Macintosh and, instead of playing the regular startup sound, it played you a little tune.

A strange startup sound usually indicates a hardware problem with RAM, video display, or a SCSI device. In rare cases, it could be a problem with the System file.

Read the Sad Mac Message

A black screen with a sad Macintosh face in it is another indication of serious problems. Look at the two rows of hexadecimal numbers beneath the Sad Mac and compare the top row with these for a possible answer:

Top Row Number	Possible Problem
00000000	RAM Chip Problem
00000001	ROM Chip Problem
00000002	RAM Chip Problem
00000003	RAM Chip Problem
00000004	RAM Chip Problem
00000005	RAM Chip Problem
00000006	VIA1 Chip Problem
00000007	VIA2 Chip Problem
00000008	Bus Problem

Top Row Number	Possible Problem
00000009	MMU Chip Problem
0000000A	Disk Partition Map Problem (You may be able to solve this by updating the disk driver.)
0000000B	SCSI Chip Problem
0000000C	Floppy Controller Problem
0000000D	SCC Chip Problem
0000000E	Data Bus or SIMM Problem
0000000F	Hardware failure during software request problem. (You may be able to solve this by replacing the System file.)

As you can see from this table, a Sad Mac is indeed bad news. Pull out the phone book and call your nearest authorized Apple repair center for help.

Understand the Question Mark Icon

You started your Macintosh but the desktop didn't appear. Instead, you see a flashing question mark icon like the one in Figure 9.3.

The question mark icon normally indicates that your Macintosh can't find the System file. The reason why it can't find the System file determines how serious the problem is.

♦ If your Macintosh can't find the System file because there's no System file on the disk, boot from another disk.

♦ If your Macintosh can't find the System file because the System file is corrupted, simply reinstall the System.

♦ If your Macintosh can't find the System file because it can't read the hard disk, you may have a serious problem. First check all connections. (If it's an internal disk, chances are the connections

Figure 9.3 The question mark icon

are okay unless you just finished messing with them.) If the connections are fine, try using disk diagnosis and repair software to solve the problem. If the disk is gone for good, specialized repair software may not even be able to "see" the disk.

♦ On some systems, a question mark icon might appear if more than one SCSI device in the chain has the same SCSI ID number.

Use a Bootable Floppy

When you get a question mark icon at startup, that means your Macintosh *can* run—it just doesn't have the right software to get started. Any floppy disk that contains a System file and application file can be used as a bootable floppy. Your Disk Tools disk is a good candidate. The "emergency" disks that come with programs like Symantec's *Norton Utilities for Macintosh* and Central Point Software's *MacTools* may be even better.

As soon as you insert a bootable floppy, the question mark should disappear. After a moment, your Macintosh's desktop should appear. (This might take a while, especially if the floppy has System 7 on it, since floppies take longer to read than hard disks. Be patient.) Once you're in the Finder, you can start tracking down the problem.

Look for Your Hard Disk Icon

If you got the question mark icon at startup but you can see your hard disk icon when you boot from a floppy, breathe a sign of relief. This means your hard disk has not crashed and you can probably still use it. If your hard disk does not appear on the desktop, however, it's time to use disk diagnosis and repair software to find it.

Cure Bombs During Startup

If your Macintosh seems to start properly but bombs as extension and control panel icons are being displayed across the bottom of the screen, you probably have a bad extension or control panel or a conflict. Pay attention to the icon that is displayed when the bomb occurs. Chances are, the program with that icon or the one that loads right after it is the problem. Remove it and start again.

Eject a Disk at Startup

If you've got a bootable floppy disk in your disk drive but it bombs the system every time you start, you may be wondering how you can get it out. There are two ways:

♦ Use a disk ejection tool. What? You didn't get one of these with your Macintosh? Don't worry—no one did. Take a paper clip and straighten it. Poke one end into the tiny hole to the side of the disk drive. You should be able to push back a lever there. *Never* do this while your Macintosh is running since a poke in the wrong place could cause a short. In fact, although disk ejection tools are widely used, they're really not such a good idea.

♦ Hold down your mouse button as you start (or restart) your Macintosh. If the drive is functioning properly, the disk should eject itself.

Disk Diagnosis and Repair Software Tricks

Be prepared. That's not just a motto scouts use. When your Macintosh starts acting strangely or files start disappearing, you'll want to be prepared to solve problems quickly.

That's where disk diagnosis and repair software come in. These software products check disks or your entire system and repair or provide information on any problems they find. Some of these packages are so powerful that they can even recover files you deleted on purpose by accident.

Use Disk First Aid

Disk First Aid is provided on the Disk Tools disk that comes with the Macintosh System software. It's designed to verify the directory structure of most hard and floppy disks. If Disk First Aid finds problems, you can use it to try to repair them. Here's how you use it.

❶ Launch Disk First Aid. Its window, which is illustrated in Figure 9.4, displays all mounted volumes, an information window with instructions, and three buttons.

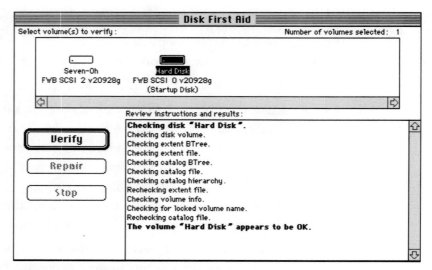

Figure 9.4 The Disk First Aid window

2 Choose the volume you want to check by clicking its icon in the top of the window. It becomes selected. To select more than one disk, hold down **Shift** while clicking on each one.

3 Click **Verify** to check the disk. The information window displays the progress of the check. This process can take a few minutes if the disk is large.

4 The results of the check and any additional information appears at the bottom of the window when the verification process is finished.

If the disk has a problem, you can use the **Repair** button to try to fix it. Disk First Aid may or may not be able to fix the problem. Disk First Aid cannot repair a locked disk or the startup disk.

Use MacCheck

MacCheck is another free Apple diagnosis tool. You can find it on the Macintosh Software Utility Update disk discussed in Chapter 3 if it didn't come with your Macintosh.

MacCheck helps you learn more about your Macintosh computer and can help diagnose software problems that may be caused by corrupted

If Your Disk First Aid Looks Different

If, after selecting a disk to check, your copy of Disk First Aid looks like the one in Figure 9.5, you don't have the most current version. The one discussed above is version 7.2, which is available on the Macintosh System Update 3.0 discussed in Chapter 3.

If you don't have the latest version and you've got a problem, don't panic. The older version should work just as well as its redesigned descendent. Click **Start** to begin the check and wait for the "Test done" message. To display the details of the testing—press **Command-S** (for "Scavenge") to display a window like the one in Figure 9.6.

files and directories. It creates a profile of your computer that includes information about its processor, memory, expansion cards, and connected devices, as well as installed software on your startup disk. MacCheck can also perform tests of the logic board, check the file directories and System file for corruption, and locate duplicate System folders. Here's how to use it:

1. Launch MacCheck. As it starts up, it begins gathering information about your System. It displays it progress in its splash screen, which is illustrated in Figure 9.7. Be patient, the startup process can take several minutes, depending on the speed and complexity of your system.

2. When MacCheck's main screen (illustrated in Figure 9.8) appears, click **Test** to have MacCheck perform tests on your hardware and System files. These tests take a few minutes. As

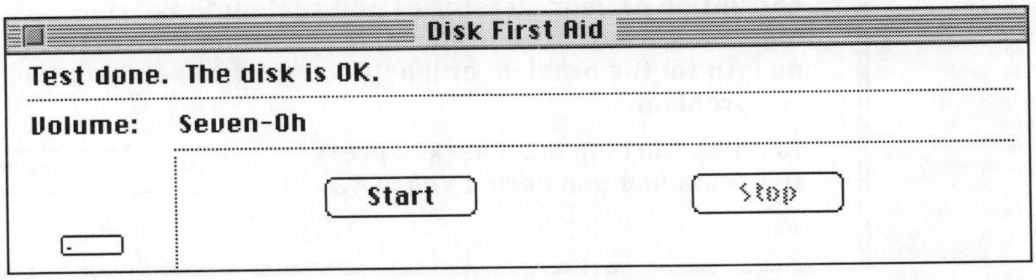

Figure 9.5 The "old" version of Disk First Aid

```
4/29/94  6:17:34 PM: Scavenging begun.

Checking disk volume.
Checking extent BTree.
Checking extent file.
Checking catalog BTree.
Checking catalog file.
Checking catalog hierarchy.
Checking volume info.
Scavenging terminated.

4/29/94  6:18:00 PM: Scavenging ended.
```

Figure 9.6 The "Scavenge" window

the tests are done, their results appear in MacCheck's main scrolling window.

3 Click the **System Info** button (or press **Command-I**) to get information about your Macintosh's hardware. Some of the information MacCheck provides is very technical. You can get more hardware information by choosing **Additional System Info** from the **Windows** menu.

4 Choose **Application and Font Info** from the **Windows** menu to view a detailed list of installed fonts and applications. One of the great things about MacCheck is that it identifies whether an application is 32-bit clean. If you're running your Macintosh in 32-bit mode and have trouble with a specific application, this can tell you why.

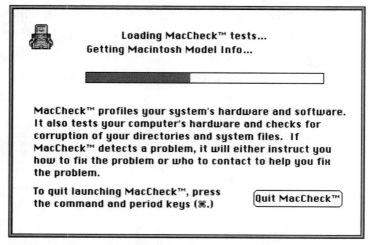

Figure 9.7 MacCheck's splash screen

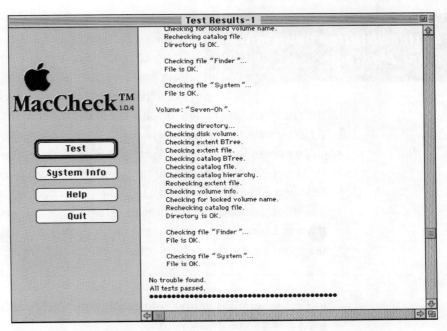

Figure 9.8 MacCheck's main screen after a test

⑤ To save the results of a test, including all the information Mac-Check has gathered, choose **Save Results** (**Command-S**) from the **File** menu. The resulting text document can be opened by MacCheck or any word processing application.

Miscellaneous Troubleshooting Tricks

• •

Here are a few more troubleshooting tricks you might find useful when working with your Macintosh.

Increase Application RAM

An application's RAM allocation is the amount of RAM allocated to it by the System to run. Chapter 4 discussed application RAM in detail. When a program has any of these problems, you should probably use the Finder's **Get Info** window to increase its RAM allocation:

♦ The program won't open as many files as you need it to.

♦ The program won't open large files, especially graphics files.

Norton Utilities and Central Point MacTools

Disk First Aid and *MacCheck* are two Apple Computer, Inc. tools that you can get for free from Apple dealers, some online services, and many user groups. They can be helpful, but they're often not enough to solve serious problems. That's when it's time to call in the heavy hitters.

Symantec Corporation's *Norton Utilities for Macintosh* and Central Point Software's *MacTools* are two similar software products that can help you when Disk First Aid can't. They can check your disks for file and directory damage, repair many problems, and even recover files that your Macintosh thinks are gone for good. No serious Macintosh user should be without one of these products or another similar product.

♦ The program is acting sluggishly, constantly reading and writing to disk as you work with it.

♦ The program displays an Out of Memory error message.

♦ The program frequently bombs when working with large files or graphics.

Cure Frequent Bombs and Error Messages

If you often get bombs, freeze-ups, and error messages in multiple applications, reinstalling your System may help. Chapter 3 provides detailed instructions for doing this correctly.

If the problems occur only in a specific application, try this:

♦ Check the software documentation to be sure your system meets the software's requirements for RAM, CPU, math co-processor, 32-bit mode, etc.

♦ Increase the application's RAM allocation using the Finder's **Get Info** window for the application. (Chapter 4 provides details.)

♦ If all else fails, delete the application and its support files and reinstall it from scratch. There's a chance that one or more files could be corrupt, causing the problem.

Back Up Your System Folder

Many software-related problems can be solved simply by replacing the System software. This can be a time-consuming process. You can reduce the amount of time it takes to replace your System by simply including the System folder in your regular backup procedure—you do back up your documents regularly, don't you? This way, replacing the System can be as easy as restoring files from a backup.

Zap the PRAM

Parameter RAM or *PRAM* is special RAM set aside to store settings for the current date and time, desktop pattern, alert sound and sound volume, keyboard and mouse settings, colors, and a number of other things. As you might have noticed, most of these things are set with control panels. PRAM uses battery power to store these settings so your Macintosh can use them when it starts up.

Although it isn't a very common problem, PRAM settings can become lost or corrupted. Indications of this include incorrect date or time, unusual font in system dialog boxes (like the **About This Macintosh** window), and settings that keep changing. You can reset the contents of PRAM, bringing your System back to default settings, by "zapping" the PRAM. Here's how.

♦ On a System 7 Macintosh, begin by quitting all applications except the Finder. Hold down **Command-Option-P-R** while choosing the **Restart** command from the **Special** menu (not an easy task). Keep the keys held down as your Macintosh starts. You'll hear a first startup sound and, after a moment, your screen will blink and you'll hear another startup sound. Let go of the keys.

♦ On a System 6 Macintosh, hold down **Command-Control-Option** while choosing **Control Panel** from the Apple menu. A dialog box appears, asking you to confirm that you want to Zap the PRAM. Click **OK**.

After zapping the PRAM, you'll have to use your control panels to reset the System settings the way you like them. Keep in mind that zapping the PRAM can also affect network settings, like those set with AppleTalk Remote Access.

If you continue to have problems with the PRAM-stored settings, replace your Macintosh's batteries.

Chapter 10

· ·

Power User
Customization Tricks

This chapter is for the folks who want to roll up their sleeves and dig right in to their Macintosh interface. In this chapter, you'll learn how to customize your Macintosh with a free program called *ResEdit*, one of the most powerful programming tools Apple ever put into the hands of nonprogrammers. Customize the Finder, the System, and applications so they work better or faster for you. Make files invisible. Add messages to the Get Info window. Become a sound thief. Find these tricks and more within the pages of this chapter.

If you don't have ResEdit, don't skip this chapter—you'll be missing out on some of the best tricks in this book. Read the chapter to learn what ResEdit can do for you. Then, when you're hooked, track down a copy and join the fun.

About ResEdit

ResEdit, the Apple Resource Editor, is a free application available through Apple dealers, some online services, and many Apple user groups. It enables you to open or create a resource fork for a file.

Let's take a few steps back. Macintosh files can have two parts or "forks:" the data fork and the resource fork. The data fork, which is present in all documents, contains information. The data fork for the word processing document containing this chapter, for example, would have the text of this chapter in it, as well as some special formatting codes that Microsoft Word (the application used to write this book) understands. The resource fork, which is present in all applications, desk accessories, control panels, and other "programs," contains *resources* or bits of programming code that can be used over and over by different routines within the program. For example, the resource fork for the Microsoft Word application contains icons, menus, dialog boxes, programming code, and a variety of other information that Word uses.

By placing reusable code in resources, programmers can:

- Avoid writing the same code over and over again within a program. If a specific dialog box is used five times, for example, the programmer doesn't need to write instructions for that dialog box five times or in five different places.

- Make a program easy to localize for different countries. For example, to change the menus to Spanish, simply change the menu resources.

- Make a program easy to modify for updates or customization. Since each resource can be modified, added, or deleted at any time, programs are easy to change.

That final point is what makes ResEdit such a popular software tool for nonprogrammers. With ResEdit and a little knowledge, you can customize the Finder, the System, or just about any program.

Don't Let ResEdit Zap You!

🚫 ResEdit is a potentially dangerous application. With it, you can modify files to the point where they will no longer function or cannot be read.
Never, never, *never* use ResEdit on your only copy of a file or on an original program disk. Doing so is just plain stupid. Don't be stupid. Back up your files *before* opening them with ResEdit.

File Attribute Tricks

• •

Every Macintosh file has attributes or settings that are part of the file. These include things like the name, type, and creator, creation and modification date and time, Finder flags, and label. ResEdit's **File Info** dialog box, which is illustrated in Figure 10.1, lets you view and change these settings. The following section contains a few related tips you might find useful.

See Invisible Files

This may come as a surprise to you, but the Finder doesn't display all the files on your disks. Some files, like the Desktop files and support files

```
╔══════════════ Info for Desktop ══════════════╗
║                                                ║
║   File: Desktop                     ☐ Locked   ║
║                                                ║
║   Type: FNDR    Creator: ERIK                  ║
║                                                ║
║   ☐ File Locked    ☐ Resources Locked    File In Use: No ║
║   ☐ Printer Driver MultiFinder Compatible    File Protected: No ║
║                                                ║
║   Created: Sun, Apr 17, 1994    Time: 8:38:13 PM ║
║                                                ║
║   Modified: Fri, Jan 1, 1904    Time: 12:00:00 AM ║
║      Size:  273602 bytes in resource fork      ║
║             0 bytes in data fork               ║
║   ────────────────────────────────────────    ║
║   Finder Flags: ◉ 7.ⁿ ○ 6.0.ⁿ                  ║
║     ☐ Has BNDL      ☐ No INITs    Label: None  ║
║     ☐ Shared        ☐ Inited      ☒ Invisible  ║
║     ☐ Stationery    ☐ Alias       ☐ Use Custom Icon ║
╚════════════════════════════════════════════════╝
```

Figure 10.1 ResEdit's File Info dialog box

created by some applications, are invisible. Fortunately, ResEdit (as well as a few other applications) lets you see them. Give this a try:

1 Choose **Get File/Folder Info** from ResEdit's **File** menu. (This exercise should also work with the **Open** and **Verify** commands under the **File** menu—any command that displays the **Open** dialog box within ResEdit.)

2 Use the directory portion of the standard **Open** dialog box that appears to navigate to your hard disk so that the scrolling window displays a list of its contents. Figure 10.2 shows an example.

Notice anything you don't normally see? If you're running System 7, you should see the Desktop DB and Desktop DF files that make up the "Desktop" file. (System 6 users will just see a single Desktop file.) You might also see invisible files created by programs like Adobe Systems' ATM, Symantec's Norton Utilities for Macintosh, and Aladdin System's StuffIt SpaceSaver. These are all examples of invisible files. They're invisible for a reason: so that you don't mess with them.

Make Files Invisible

Out of sight, out of mind. You can use ResEdit to cook up your own mini security system. Simply make the files you want prying eyes to keep away from invisible.

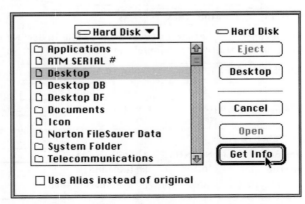

Figure 10.2 Use ResEdit to see invisible files.

① Choose **Get File/Folder Info** from ResEdit's **File** menu.

② Use the directory portion of the standard **Open** dialog box that appears to locate the file you want to make invisible.

③ Click **Get Info**.

④ In the **File Info** window that appears (see Figure 10.1) click the check box to turn **Invisible** on.

⑤ Click the close box to close the **File Info** window. When asked to save changes, click **Yes**.

Back in the Finder, the icon will be gone. If you try to open the document from within an application, it won't appear in the directory portion of the **Open** dialog box. In fact, it'll be downright tough to find it without ResEdit.

To open the file, of course, you'll have to make it visible again. Follow Steps 1 through 5 above, but turn the **Invisible** check box off in Step 4 to make the file visible again.

Make Folders Invisible

If you want to secure multiple files using the above trick, you might find it easier to simply make an entire folder full of files invisible. Use the steps above, but get info for a Folder instead of the separate files. The **Folder Info** window that appears (see Figure 10.3) offers fewer options but works the same way.

Delete the Invisible Desktop File

If you've upgraded from System 6 to System 7 and haven't formatted your hard disk since, chances are you'll have Desktop files in both System 6 and System 7 formats. If you don't plan on using System 6 again, you can delete the System 6 format Desktop file, freeing up space you probably didn't even realize was in use. Here's how:

Figure 10.3 ResEdit's Folder Info window

1 Choose **Get File/Folder Info** from ResEdit's **File** menu.

2 Use the directory portion of the standard **Open** dialog box that appears to navigate to your hard disk so that the scrolling window displays a list of its contents.

3 Locate the file named Desktop and click it to select it. This is shown in Figure 10.2. Do *not* select Desktop DB or Desktop DF—these are the System 7 Desktop files! If you cannot find a file named Desktop, click cancel and skip the rest of these steps—you don't have a System 6 Desktop file.

4 Click **Get Info**.

5 In the **File Info** window that appears (see Figure 10.1) click the check box to turn **Invisible** off. (Note also in Figure 10.1 that the file on this particular system is a whopping 273,602 bytes!)

6 Click the close box to close the **File Info** window. When asked to save changes, click **Yes**.

7 Open your hard disk icon. A plain document icon called Desktop should be among the other icons there. Drag this icon to the Trash and choose **Empty Trash** from the **Special** menu to get rid of it.

Change Type and Creator Codes

ResEdit's File Info window also displays type and creator codes for files. (You can see this in Figure 10.1.) These codes, which are part of every Macintosh file, identify the type of file and the application that created it. This information is used by the Desktop file. It determines what icon appears for a file and what application opens it when you double-click it.

In order to change the type or creator codes, you need to know what you want to change it to. Choose **Get File/Folder Info** from ResEdit's **File** menu see the type and creator codes of a file that already has the codes you want to use. Then choose **Get File/Folder Info** from the **File** menu again to enter those codes into the file you want to change. Depending on the change you make, the file's icon many change.

Why Change Type and Creator Codes?

Why would you want to change a file's type or creator code? Here are some reasons:

- You want to be able to open a plain text document in your favorite word processor when you double-click it.

- You want to be able to open a plain PICT document in your favorite graphics application when you double-click it.

- You want to convert a regular TeachText document into a read only TeachText document.

- The type or creator code is incorrect and you need to fix it.

- When you double-click the file, you get a message saying your Macintosh can't open it because the application that created it can't be found. You want to know what application created it.

The following table provides some common type and creator codes you might find useful. Remember that type and creator codes are case sensitive—be sure to enter them correctly.

Type	Creator	Description
APPL		Application
TEXT		Plain text document
PICT		Plain PICT document
TEXT	ttxt	Regular TeachText or SimpleText document
ttro	ttxt	Read-only TeachText or SimpleText document
	MSWD	Microsoft Word
	MWPR	Claris MacWrite Pro
	XCEL	Microsoft Excel
	dPro	Claris MacDraw Pro
	SPNT	Aldus SuperPaint
	FMPR	Claris FileMaker Pro
	BOBO	ClarisWorks
	XPR3	QuarkXPress
	PPT3	Microsoft PowerPoint

Changing Type and Creator Codes Doesn't Change Document Contents

Don't think that changing a document's type and creator code is all you need to do to convert one application's document format to another's. Even if you change both type and creator codes, the actual contents of the file will determine whether the file can be read properly by the application you open it with. Most programs include header information in their document files that provide instructions that may not be recognized by other programs. So if you change a Microsoft Word document to a ClarisWorks word processing document just by changing these codes, don't be surprised if you get less than perfect results.

Menu Tricks

You'll find menus in just about any Macintosh application. That means ResEdit can open and edit MENU resources in almost any application. Use ResEdit to add, change, or remove keyboard shortcuts, change command names, and colorize your menus, like the one in Figure 10.4. This section tells you how.

Don't Distribute Altered Copyrighted Software

Changing the way copyrighted applications work on your Macintosh is fine, but distributing altered copies is illegal. Don't make alterations to copyrighted software and share them with your friends or work associates. Doing so is most likely in violation of the licensing agreement you accepted when you began using the software. If you're caught, you can get into big trouble.

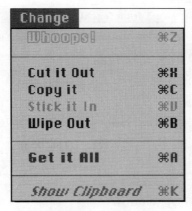

Figure 10.4 TeachText's
Edit menu after some
"ResEditing"

Add Keyboard Shortcuts

As discussed way back in Chapter 1, keyboard shortcuts make it quick
and easy to access menu commands. Commercial utility programs like
CE Software's *QuicKeys* and Now Software's *NowMenus* enable you to
add and change keyboard shortcuts, but they must be installed for the
shortcuts to work. *ResEdit* lets you add permanent shortcuts to menus.

1 Choose **Open** (**Command-O**) from ResEdit's **File** menu.

2 Use the standard **Open** dialog box that appears to open the application file you want to change. (Make sure you do not open
and change the only copy of the file!)

3 Scroll through the resource types to find the one called
MENU. Double-click it to open it.

4 In the resource picker window that appears, double-click on
the menu you want to change. The menu editor window that
appears should look something like the one in Figure 10.5.

5 Click on the name of the command you want to add a shortcut
to.

6 In the **Cmd-Key** edit box, type in the character you want to
use in conjunction with the **Command** key to choose that
command.

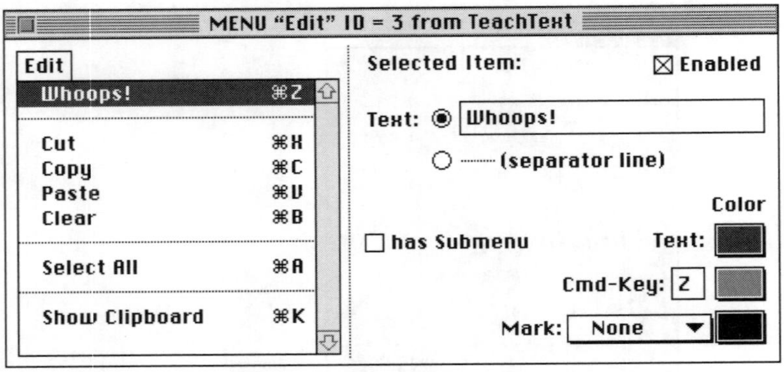

> MENU "Edit" ID = 3 from TeachText
>
> | Edit | |
> |------|---|
> | **Whoops!** | ⌘Z |
> | | |
> | Cut | ⌘X |
> | Copy | ⌘C |
> | Paste | ⌘V |
> | Clear | ⌘B |
> | | |
> | Select All | ⌘A |
> | | |
> | Show Clipboard | ⌘K |
>
> Selected Item: ☒ Enabled
>
> Text: ◉ | Whoops! |
>
> ○ ──── (separator line)
>
> Color
>
> ☐ has Submenu   Text: ▮
>
> Cmd-Key: | Z | ▮
>
> Mark: | None   ▼ | ▮

Figure 10.5 The menu editor window

7 Repeat Steps 5 and 6 for each of the commands you want to add a shortcut to.

8 Close the menu editor window.

9 Repeat Steps 4 through 8 for each of the menus you want to add shortcuts to.

10 Choose **Save** (**Command-S**) from the **File** menu to save changes.

11 Close all document windows.

The next time you launch that application, the shortcuts you specified are displayed and can be used.

Here are a few additional pointers for using this trick:

♦ Don't use a key that is used for another command. If two commands use the same keyboard shortcut, the application will use the command it finds first with that shortcut.

♦ You can remove a keyboard shortcut by deleting the contents of the **Cmd-Key** edit box in Step 6 above.

♦ You can change a keyboard shortcut by typing over the contents of the **Cmd-Key** edit box in Step 6 above.

Change Command Names

If adding shortcuts isn't enough for you, you can also change the name of a command on a menu.

1 Choose **Open** (**Command-O**) from ResEdit's **File** menu.

2 Use the standard **Open** dialog box that appears to open the application file you want to change. (Make sure you do not open and change the only copy of the file!)

3 Scroll through the resource types to find the one called **MENU**. Double-click it to open it.

4 In the resource picker window that appears, double-click on the menu you want to change. The menu editor window that appears should look something like the one in Figure 10.5.

5 Click on the name of the command you want to change.

6 In the **Text** edit box, type in a new command name.

7 Repeat Steps 5 and 6 for each of the commands you want to change.

8 Close the menu editor window.

9 Repeat Steps 4 through 8 for each of the menus you want to change.

10 Choose **Save** (**Command-S**) from the **File** menu to save changes.

11 Close all document windows.

The next time you launch that application, the command names you specified are displayed under each menu.

Here are a few additional ideas for this trick:

♦ Change the name of the menu itself by clicking on the menu name and typing a new name into the **Text** edit box in Step 6 above.

♦ Choose a style for a menu command or menu name by clicking on it to select it (in Step 5 above) and choosing a style from the **Style** menu.

♦ If the file includes ICON or SICN resources, you can place icons in front of menu commands by choosing **Choose Icon** from the **MENU** menu and selecting the icon you want to use. If the file doesn't have ICON or SICN resources, you can add them.

Colorize Your Menus

If your Macintosh supports color, you might want to brighten your menus up a bit. Here's how.

1 Choose **Open** (**Command-O**) from ResEdit's **File** menu.

2 Use the standard **Open** dialog box that appears to open the application file you want to change. (Make sure you do not open and change the only copy of the file!)

3 Scroll through the resource types to find the one called **MENU**. Double-click it to open it.

4 In the resource picker window that appears, double-click on the menu you want to change. The menu editor window that appears should look something like the one in Figure 10.5.

5 Click on the name of the command you want to colorize.

6 Click on the color box beside **Text** to display a menu of available colors and choose one. This changes the color of the text in the menu. If this is the first time a menu has been colorized, a warning dialog box may appear, telling you that an mctb resource will be created. Click **OK**.

7 Click on the color box beside **Cmd-Key** to display a menu of colors and choose one. This changes the color of the command key indicator for that command in the menu.

8 If the menu has a marker to indicate whether it's turned on or off, click on the color box beside **Mark** to display a menu of colors and choose one. This changes the color of the marker for that menu.

9 Repeat Steps 5 through 8 for each of the commands you want to colorize.

10 Close the menu editor window.

11 Repeat Steps 4 through 10 for each of the menus you want to colorize.

12 Choose **Save** (**Command-S**) from the **File** menu to save changes.

13 Close all document windows.

The next time you launch that application, the menus you colorized appear in color.

Finder and System Customization Tricks

The Finder and System files are full of very special resources—resources that are used by other applications. That means you can customize many applications just by customizing a few Finder or System resources.

Although editing the Finder and System files are not recommended, here are a few relatively harmless tricks you can try.

How to Edit the Finder and System Files

There's a trick to editing the Finder and System files without doing permanent damage.

Be sure to read this sidebar before opening either file with ResEdit!

- Since ResEdit cannot edit an active Finder, your best bet is to start your Macintosh with a bootable floppy or a System folder on another mounted volume. Duplicate the Finder and place the Finder Copy in another folder for safekeeping. Then edit the original Finder file with ResEdit. When you're finished and have saved your changes, restart your Macintosh. The Finder that launches at startup should be the edited one. Don't delete the Finder Copy , just in case the edited one turns out to be bad.

- Although you can edit the active System file, it isn't recommended—it can cause system bombs and permanently corrupt your System file. The trouble is, it's also a bad idea to have more than one System file on a disk. So here's what you do: Make a copy of the System file and edit that. Then copy the unaltered System file to a floppy disk or use file compression software to compress it so it's saved in another format on the same disk. Drag the unaltered System file out of the System Folder and into the Trash. Drag the edited System Copy to the System Folder and rename it System. Restart your Macintosh. If all goes well, the edited copy of the System will be recognized and used for Startup.

Change "Welcome to Macintosh"

The "Welcome to Macintosh" message appears on your screen—provided you don't have a StartUpScreen installed—whenever you start your Macintosh. The information in this screen is stored in a Resource inside your System file. You can use ResEdit to change it.

1 Choose **Open** (**Command-O**) from ResEdit's **File** menu.

2 Use the standard **Open** dialog box that appears to open the System file. (You've already backed it up, right?)

3 Scroll through the resource types to find the one called **DSAT**. Double-click it to open it.

4 In the resource picker window that appears, locate number **0** and double-click it to open it.

5 The editor window appears. It should look something like Figure 10.6. Use the scroll bar to scroll down until you see "Welcome to Macintosh" in the right column. Use your mouse pointer to highlight this text since you will be replacing it.

6 Type in the new message. For best results, it should be exactly 21 characters long, including the period at the end. If your message is shorter than that, add spaces to the end to pad it out. If your message is not exactly 21 characters long, the Macintosh icon (which is stored in cicn resource –16396) may not appear in the window with the message.

7 Choose **Save** (**Command-S**) from the **File** menu to save your changes.

```
▤▤▤    DSAT ID = 0 from System copy    ▤▤▤
000068    B176 0000 BFF0 0000    ±v□□●□□□    ⬆
000070    AA0F B17B 001A 006C    ™□± {□□□ I
000078    00C0 5765 6C63 6F6D    □¿Welcom
000080    6520 746F 204D 6163    e to Mac
000088    696E 746F 7368 2E00    intosh. □
000090    B17A 0018 007E 00C0    ±z□□□▲
000098    4465 6275 6767 6572    Debugger
0000A0    2069 6E73 7461 6C6C     install
0000A8    6564 2E00 B177 0014    ed.□±w□□
0000B0    007E 00C0 4578 7465    □˜□¿Exte
0000B8    6E73 696F 6E73 206F    nsions o
0000C0    6666 2E00 B179 00CA    ff.□±y□
0000C8    005E 0072 5468 6973    □^□rThis    ⬇
0000D0    2073 7461 7274 7570     startup    ▤
```

Figure 10.6 Changing "Welcome to Macintosh"

8 Choose **Quit** (**Command-Q**) from the **File** menu to quit ResEdit.

When you restart your Macintosh with the edited System file active, your message should appear in place of "Welcome to Macintosh."

Change the Trash Name

Ever notice that you can't rename the Trash from within the Finder? You can from within ResEdit.

1 Choose **Open** (**Command-O**) from ResEdit's **File** menu.

2 Use the standard **Open** dialog box that appears to open the Finder file. (You've already backed it up, right?)

3 Scroll through the resource types to find the one called **STR#**. Double-click it to open it.

4 In the resource picker window that appears, locate number **11750** and double-click it to open it.

5 The editor window opens. It should look something like the one in Figure 10.7. Enter a new name for the Trash in the first edit box.

6 Close the editor window.

7 Choose **Save** (**Command-S**) from the File menu to save changes.

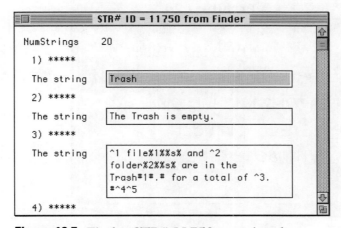

Figure 10.7 Finder STR# 11750 contains the name of the Trash.

8 Choose **Quit** (**Command-Q**) from the File menu to quit Res-Edit.

When you restart your Macintosh with the edited Finder file active, your Trash icon will have a new name.

Change the Name of the Trash Everywhere!

Finder STR# 11750 contains all the strings used in Trash-related dialog boxes. If you change the name of the Trash on your System, why not change the text that goes in related dialog boxes? Just replace the word Trash with the name you're using in all strings of this resource. You'll see your changes in menus and dialog boxes throughout the system.

Change the Font Sample Text

When you double-click on the icon for a bitmapped or TrueType font, a window with some sample text in that font is displayed. You can change this sample text with ResEdit. Figure 10.8 shows an example of what you can do.

1 Choose **Open** (**Command-O**) from ResEdit's **File** menu.

2 Use the standard **Open** dialog box that appears to open the Finder file. (You've already backed it up, right?)

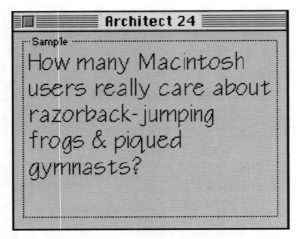

Figure 10.8 Make the Font sample text say almost anything you like.

3 Scroll through the resource types to find the one called **STR#**. Double-click it to open it.

4 In the resource picker window that appears, locate number **14516** and double-click it to open it.

5 The editor window opens. An edit box displays the standard sample text: "How razorback-jumping frogs..." Replace this text with text you want to see in the font sample window.

6 Close the editor window.

7 Choose **Save** (**Command-S**) from the **File** menu to save changes.

8 Choose **Quit** (**Command-Q**) from the **File** menu to quit Res-Edit.

When you restart your Macintosh with the edited Finder file active and double-click a font icon, the text you specified appears in the sample.

Customize the Desktop Pattern

The General control panel offers a basic way to change your desktop pattern: Edit the pixels in its window and then click on the miniature desktop to lock them in. You can go a step further with ResEdit to create more complex desktop pattern images like the sample in Figure 10.9.

1 Choose **Open** (**Command-O**) from ResEdit's **File** menu.

2 Use the standard **Open** dialog box that appears to open the System file. (You've already backed it up, right?)

3 Scroll through the resource types to find the one called **ppat**. Double-click it to open it.

4 In the resource picker window that appears, there should be only one resource inside: **16**. Double-click it to open it.

5 The pixel editor window, which is shown in Figure 10.10, opens. It contains an 8 x 8 pixel image of the desktop pattern. This is the same size as the desktop pattern editor offered in the General control panel.

Figure 10.9 Cab
Calloway can be on
your desktop, too.

6 To increase the size of the pattern, choose **Pattern Size** from
the **ppat** menu. The **Pattern Size** dialog box, which is shown
in Figure 10.11, appears. Select a larger square pattern. (The
larger the pattern, the more detail you can include in your desktop pattern.) Click **Resize** to change the size and close the dialog box.

7 Back in the pixel editor window, use the tools, color palettes,
and pattern palettes to create your masterpiece. You can choose
Try Pattern from the **ppat** menu at any time to see the results
of your efforts.

8 When you're finished, choose **Save** (**Command-S**) from the
File menu to save changes.

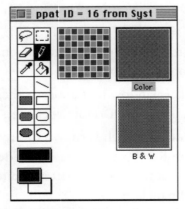

Figure 10.10 The ppat
pixel editor

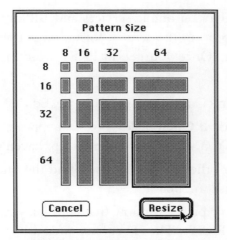

Figure 10.11 The Pattern Size
dialog box

9 Choose **Quit** (**Command-Q**) from the **File** menu to quit Res-
Edit.

When you restart your Macintosh with the edited System file active,
you'll see your custom desktop pattern.

Paste in a ppat

What? You're no artist? Fortunately, there are artists out there who like
to share their ppats with us. That's where the Cab Calloway example in
Figure 10.9 came from. Check online services and local BBSes for ppat
files. Open them with ResEdit and paste them into your System file. Be
sure it's assigned resource ID 16 when pasting it in. (You can change a
resource ID number by choosing **Get Resource Info** from the **Resource** menu when the resource is selected.)

Add FKEYs

FKEYs are tiny programs that you install in your System file and access
with **Command-Shift-number key** combinations. Apple has four
built-in FKEYs, which were covered in Chapter 1. They use the Com-
mand-Shift-1, Command-Shift-2, Command-Shift-3, and Command-
Shift-0 key combinations. That leaves you with 4 through 9 for your
own.

You can find FKEYs on online services and BBSes. They perform a variety of tasks: capturing the screen, formatting clipboard text, quitting the Finder, etc. Once you get an FKEY, you'll need to install it. Here's how.

1 Choose **Open** (**Command-O**) from ResEdit's **File** menu.

2 Use the standard **Open** dialog box that appears to open the System file. (You've already backed it up, haven't you?)

3 Scroll through the resource types to find the one called **FKEY**. Double-click it to open it.

4 In the resource picker window that appears, you should see all the installed FKEYs. The ID corresponds to the number key you need to press with **Command** and **Shift** to activate the FKEY. If you have not added any FKEYs to your System file, there should be only one: ID **3**.

5 Choose **Open** (**Command-O**) from the **File** menu.

6 Use the standard **Open** dialog box that appears to open the document containing the FKEY you want to install.

7 You should see an icon for **FKEY** resources. Double-click it to open it. The resource picker displays all the FKEYs in the file. There may be only one.

8 Click on the ID for the FKEY you want to install to select it.

9 Choose **Copy** (**Command-C**) from the **Edit** menu.

10 Click on the System file's FKEY resource picker window to make it the active window.

11 Choose **Paste** (**Command-V**) from the **Edit** menu. The FKEY is pasted into your System file. If a dialog box appears asking if you want to replace resources with the same ID, click **Unique ID** to have ResEdit assign a different ID number (usually 128). Then choose **Get Resource Info** from the **Resource** menu to change the ID to an unused number between 4 and 9.

12 Choose **Save** (**Command-S**) from the **File** menu to save changes.

13 Choose **Quit** (**Command-Q**) from the **File** menu to quit Res-Edit.

When you restart your Macintosh with the edited System file active, you'll be able to use your new FKEY.

Remap Keyboard Keys

It's four o'clock on a Friday afternoon and you're on United Flight 67 from Chicago. Your PowerBook is on your tray table and you're working frantically on a report your secretary will pick up at the airport. After handing it over on disk, you're going to hop onto Flight 329 to Honolulu for a two-week vacation in paradise. Suddenly, your K key stops working. No matter what you do, you can't get your keyboard to produce the letter K. What do you do?

If you have ResEdit handy, you can remap the Keyboard so that the K key can be accessed by pressing another key, like the ' or \ key. Here's how:

1 Choose **Open** (**Command-O**) from ResEdit's **File** menu.

2 Use the standard **Open** dialog box that appears to open the System file. (You've already backed it up, right?)

3 Scroll through the resource types to find the one called **KCHR**. Double-click it to open it.

4 In the resource picker window that appears, click once on the name of the keyboard layout you are using to select it.

5 Choose **Duplicate** (**Command-D**) from the **Edit** menu. This copies the keyboard layout so you can easily switch back to the original once the key is fixed. If desired, choose **Get Resource Info** from the **Resource** menu and give the resource a new name. Then close the **Resource Info** window.

6 Double-click the copy of the keyboard layout to open it. The main KCHR editor window appears. It looks like the one in Figure 10.12.

7 With **Table 0** selected on the far right side of the window, find the letter **k** (lowercase) in the large box of keyboard characters on the left side of the window. Use your mouse to drag the **k**

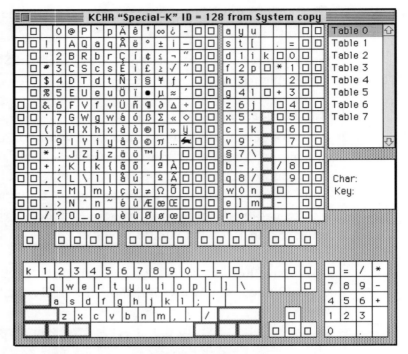

Figure 10.12 The main KCHR editor window

to the keyboard layout of characters below it and drop the **k** onto the keyboard key you want to use to type *k*. This maps the lowercase *k* to that keyboard key.

8 Click on **Table 1** on the far right side of the window. Click **OK** in the confirmation dialog box that appears. Find the letter **K** (uppercase) in the large box of keyboard characters on the left side of the window. Use your mouse to drag the **K** to the same keyboard key you used for the lowercase character. This maps the uppercase *K* to that keyboard key when the shift key is pressed.

9 Choose **Save** (**Command-S**) from the **File** menu to save changes.

10 Choose **Quit** (**Command-Q**) from the **File** menu to quit Res-Edit.

11 Restart your Macintosh with the edited System file active.

12 Use the **Keyboard** control panel to select the new keyboard layout you edited. When you press the key you remapped the character to, the character appears on your screen.

Miscellaneous ResEdit Tricks

ResEdit has a lot more tricks up its sleeve. Here are a few of the more interesting ones.

Check Resources

ResEdit automatically performs a partial test of resources when it opens a file. If it finds a problem, it performs a full test. To force ResEdit to perform a full test of every file it opens:

1 Choose **Preferences** from the **File** menu.

2 In the **Preferences** dialog box that appears (see Figure 10.13), turn on the check box for **Verify files when they are opened**.

3 Click **OK**.

Once this is turned on, ResEdit will display a progress box as it verifies each file it opens.

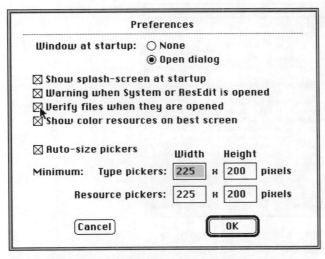

Figure 10.13 ResEdit's Preferences dialog box

Verify Only Certain Files

If you don't want to verify every single file, keep the **Verify files as they are opened** check box turned off in the **Preferences** dialog box. Instead, choose the **Verify** command from the **File** menu to verify a file you select. The same progress box will appear.

Add Version Info to Files

Most applications have version numbers. They are displayed in the Finder's Get Info window, as illustrated in Figure 10.14. Version numbers are stored in vers resources. You can use ResEdit to edit them or to add vers resources to files that don't have them—even document files! This is a great way to add "comments" that aren't lost when you rebuild your desktop.

1 Choose **Open** (**Command-O**) from ResEdit's **File** menu.

2 Use the standard **Open** dialog box that appears to open the file you want to edit. (Make sure you do not open and change the only copy of the file!)

3 If the file is a document, it may not have a resource fork. In that case, you'll see a dialog box telling you that to open the document, ResEdit will add a resource fork. Click **OK**.

Figure 10.14 The Get Info window displays version information in two places.

④ Look for a resource type named **vers**. If you find it, double-click it to open it. Then double-click the resource with an ID of **1** to open it. If there are no **vers** resources, choose **Create New Resource** (**Command-K**) from the **Resource** menu. In the scrolling list of resource types, choose **vers** and click **OK**. ResEdit creates a new vers resource with ID **128** and opens the vers resource editor, which is shown in Figure 10.15.

⑤ Enter the appropriate version information. The information in the bottom edit box is what appears in the Finder's **Get Info** window. When you are finished, close the editor window.

⑥ If necessary, choose **Get Resource Info** (**Command-I**) from the **Resource** menu to change the **vers** resource ID to **1**. While in the **Resource Info** window, also turn the **Purgeable** check box on. Close the **Resource Info** window when you're finished.

⑦ Follow Steps 4 through 6 to edit or create **vers** resource ID **2**.

⑧ Choose **Save** (**Command-S**) from the **File** menu to save the changes.

⑨ Choose **Quit** (**Command-Q**) from the **File** menu to quit ResEdit.

When you open the **Get Info** window for the file in the Finder, you should see the information you entered.

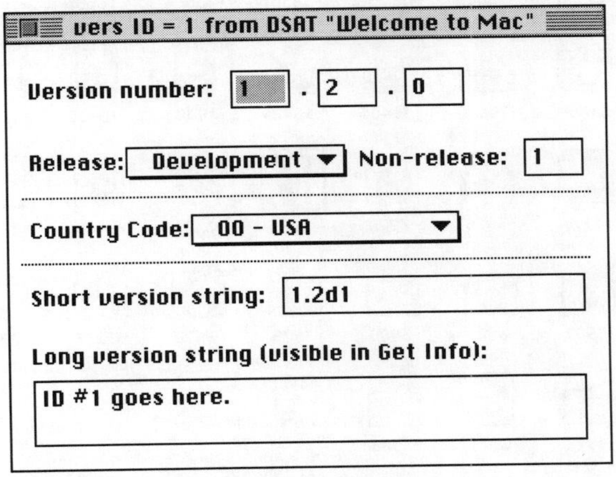

Figure 10.15 The vers editor window

Edit Icons

ResEdit is probably most often used by nonprogrammers as an icon editor. If offers a number of tools that make icon editing easy. Give it a try.

1 Choose **Open** (**Command-O**) from ResEdit's **File** menu.

2 Use the standard **Open** dialog box that appears to open the file you want to edit. (Make sure you do not open and change the only copy of the file!) Don't bother opening a document file looking for an icon. All icons are stored in creator's application file or System file.

3 Look for one of the following resource types: **icl8** (256-color icon), **icl4** (16-color icon), or **ICN#** (black and white icon). Double-click on the icon for the resource you want to edit.

4 All the icons for that resource are displayed. Figure 10.16 shows all the **icl8** resources inside the System file. Double-click on the icon you want to edit.

5 The icon editor, which is illustrated in Figure 10.17, appears. Use its tools, color palettes, and pattern palette to edit the icon.

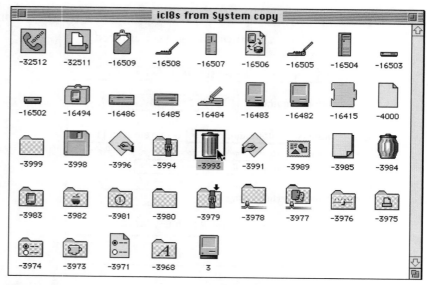

Figure 10.16 icl8 resources in the System file

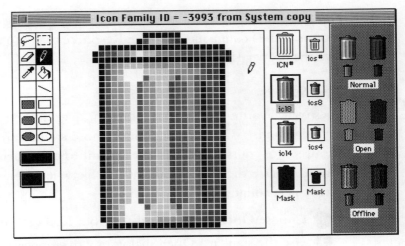

Figure 10.17 Editing the Trash icon

6 When you've finished editing one kind of icon, position your mouse pointer over it's small image on the right side of the window. There should be a dark border around it already. Drag this icon onto each of the other icon boxes on the right side of the screen, one at a time. This copies your changes to the other resources in the icon family without you having to change them all manually. Colors are adjusted accordingly (that's why it's a good idea to edit the icon with the most colors first).

7 Choose **Save** (**Command-S**)from the **File** menu to save the changes.

8 Choose **Quit** (**Command-Q**) from the **File** menu to quit Res-Edit.

The changes you made will either appear immediately or after you rebuild the Desktop.

Paste in an Icon

Just as you can paste in ppat resources (as discussed above), you can paste in various icon resources. Icons are widely available on online services and BBSes. Why spend hours fiddling around with pixel editors when you can simply paste in color icons created by artists who know what they're doing? Just remember to use the **Get Resource Info** (**Command-I**) command from the **Resource** menu to be sure the icons have the proper ID and are purgeable.

Steal Sounds

Does your favorite Macintosh shoot-'em-up arcade game make all kinds of cool sounds? Where do you think those sounds are stored? In **snd resources**, of course! You can use ResEdit to copy them out of applications and paste them into your System file where you can use them as system alert sounds. Here's how.

1 Choose **Open** (**Command-O**) from ResEdit's **File** menu.

2 Use the standard **Open** dialog box that appears to open the file containing sounds you want to steal. (Make sure you do not open and change the only copy of the file!)

3 Look for a resource type called **snd**. Double-click on its icon.

4 The resource picker that appears lists all the **snd** resources in the file. Click on one to select it and choose **Try Sound** (**Command-T**) from the **snd** menu to listen to it.

5 To copy the sound, choose **Copy** (**Command-C**) from the **Edit** menu.

6 Choose **Open** (**Command-O**) from ResEdit's **File** menu.

Hints for Sound Thieves

If you'd like to start collecting sounds but don't know where to find them other than in game files, here are some hints:

- Have you ever completed the puzzle in the Puzzle DA?
- Did you know that ResEdit can grunt like a pig?
- Do you use America Online? Or a FirstClass BBS with a really cool settings file?
- Has anyone ever asked you to turn down the sound on your screen saver?

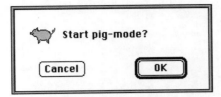

Figure 10.18 Start Pig Mode?

7 Use the standard **Open** dialog box that appears to open a copy of your System file.

8 Choose **Paste** (**Command-V**) from the **Edit** menu to paste the sound into the System file. If a dialog box appears offering to give the sound a unique ID, click **Unique ID**.

9 Repeat Steps 4, 5, and 8 to copy sounds from one file and paste them into your System file.

10 Choose **Save** (**Command-S**) from the **File** menu to save changes.

11 Choose **Quit** (**Command-Q**) from the **File** menu to quit ResEdit.

After you restart your Macintosh with the edited System file active, you can use the **Sound** control panel to select from among your new sounds.

Enter Pig Mode

What would a chapter about ResEdit be without mentioning Pig Mode?

Hold down **Command-Option-Shift** and choose **About ResEdit** from the **Apple** menu. Your Macintosh grunts and opens a dialog box like the one in Figure 10.18. Click **OK**. Your Macintosh will grunt periodically as you work. When you get tired of it, hold down **Command-Option-Shift** and choose **About ResEdit** from the **Apple** menu again. This time, the dialog box lets you turn off the oinking.

Index

A

N

O

About the Author

· ·

Maria L. Langer is a freelance writer and Macintosh consultant. She is the author of five Macintosh books and has written articles and reviews for publications like *MacWEEK*, *MacUser*, and *Data Training*.

Maria is the Publisher of *Macintosh Tips & Tricks*, a news and productivity newsletter for Macintosh Users. *Macintosh Tips & Tricks* is published in both printed and electronic formats and reaches approximately 10,000 readers each month. She is also a co-editor of *Home and School Mac*, the newsletter of the National Home & School Macintosh User's Group.

Maria is a frequent speaker at user group meetings and other Macintosh events. She's part of the MacWorld Expo faculty and speaks regularly at MacWorld Expo in Boston, San Francisco, and Toronto.

In addition to writing, editing, and speaking activities, Maria does Macintosh consulting and applications training. She also runs a Macintosh-based bulletin board system, *The Electronic Pen BBS*, which has been online continuously for over five years.

When Maria isn't working with or talking about Macs (which isn't often), she's reading or writing fiction or riding her motorcycle.

Macintosh®
Tips & Tricks™

Helping you get more out of your Macintosh every day.

Macintosh Tips & Tricks is an affordable news and productivity newsletter for Macintosh users that first appeared in subscriber mailboxes and online services in 1992. Each monthly issue is jam-packed with useful tips that help readers:

❖ save time and effort performing everyday tasks with the System software and popular applications,

❖ find out how to get the most out of hardware, software, and services,

❖ customize the Macintosh work environment to make work easier or more fun,

❖ understand how Macintosh hardware and software works, and

❖ learn about new products that can help get work done.

Macintosh Tips & Tricks is available as a printed newsletter distributed to paid subscribers and electronically as a shareware DOCMaker file distributed via online services. The printed version contains illustrations and additional articles not provided in the electronic version.

An estimated 10,000 Macintosh users read *Macintosh Tips & Tricks* each month — shouldn't **you** be one of them?

Get a Free Sample Issue!

If you liked the slick tricks in this book, you'll love getting more tips and tricks each month. Clip this coupon page, fill it out, and send it to Giles Road Press, MT&T Free Issue Offer, P.O. Box 212, Harrington Park, NJ 07640-0212 to get a free sample issue and complete subscription information.

Name: _____

Address: _____

_____

_____

E-Mail Addresses: _____

Offer expires 12/31/95 and is limited to one free issue per person or address. Original coupons only, please.